Till The Last Cut
Is Delivered . . .

Till The Last Cut Is Delivered . . .

The Poetic Anthology

Vasanth Kumar J

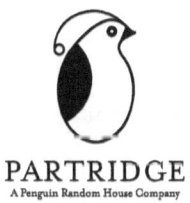

PARTRIDGE
A Penguin Random House Company

ISBN: Softcover   978-1-4828-6793-0
             eBook   978-1-4828-6792-3

To order additional copies of this book, contact
Partridge India
000 800 10062 62
orders.india@partridgepublishing.com

www.partridgepublishing.com/india

Contents

1. Cold Sale...1
2. Continue... 3
3. Decked Courage...4
4. Dial M for... 5
5. Dust Storm 6
6. Leave her be... 7
7. Line of Thought 8
8. Melodrama... 9
9. Run, child... 10
10. Silence the Sun... 11
11. Smoke Dance 12
12. Spiral Eyed...13
13. Turbulence 14
14. Deep Musings 15
15. Early Eyes 17
16. Gates 18
17. Déjà Vu 19
18. Dope Hope 20
19. Echoed In Eternity 22
20. Fading Flames 24
21. The Vagabond..25
22. For Whom the Bell Tolls..27
23. Last Smoke...30
24. Mad Train 31

25. Night Knight...33

26. Paradise Symphony 34

27. Pirate, I Am… 35

28. Pushed to hell! 37

29. Sakhi! 39

30. The Shadow Boxer...41

31. Silent Walls...42

32. Sketches in the Sky.......................................43

33. Soul Driver... 44

34. Bad To The Bone.. 46

35. Sky Reel...47

36. Paper Wings..49

37. Rewind 51

38. Chained To Pain..53

39. Dark Side Of The Moon 54

40. Kudos 56

41. Early Angel 57

42. Keep Smiling 62

43. Skin Strike 64

44. The Unsung...65

45. Unseen Nation 67

46. Smoke On The Water 69

47. Sky Tales..73

48. Dreamcatcher..76

49. Angels On Fire...80

50. Fading Black..81

51. Fallen Angel..82

52. Overture of Departure 85

53. Reach The Sky, Remember The Earth 86

54. The Homecoming 87

55. The Last Stand...92

56. The Element..96

57. Nail on the coffin...97

58. Foot-Notes 98

59. Day One Dark… 100

60. Soldier of the Sun 102

61. Mirror, Mirror On The Wall............................103

62. Dirty Money 104

63. Welcome Waters 106

64. Mother, Dear… 108

65. True That! 110

66. Final Field 111

67. Live To Die Another Day… 113

68. Storm Child 114

69. Blind Cut..116

70. Spirit Today 117

71. Rush Hour 119

72. Nothing's Lost..121

73. Open Arms 123

74. Walk on, fight on… 124

75. Impromptu...125

76. Midnight Muse...127

77. The Reunion 128

78. Closing End...129

79. V for… 130

80. U-Turn...133

81. Calling Fields 134

82. On The Edge… 136

83. My Dear Madras… 137

84. Nail the Enigma..140

Foreword

While writing the foreword for Mr. Vasanth Kumar's poetic anthology, 'Till The Last Cut Is Delivered...' I am experiencing the signature delight of a gardener who plants an insignificant sapling at the corner of a garden, affectionately nurtures it and joyously watches it growing into a towering tree with its undeniable presence in the green world. Nearly seventeen years have elapsed since I met Vasanth for the first time. That curious, imaginative young boy today takes his maiden voyage to the blissful creative world. The anthology certainly echoes a mature voice, celebrating life with unshaken hope and positivity.

'Till The Last Cut Is Delivered...' promises to unfold a budding poet's journey to visibility. The path is a unique merger of experience, thoughts and reaction. Somewhere during the journey, the poetic voice leaves the little domain of an individual and echoes the expressions of many. The wide range of themes makes the work fascinating. Freedom is denied, dream is broken, pain is muted, anger loses fire— cold deal is closed. The sight is familiar but the appeal is fresh in the novel 'script of our dear souls'. Sometimes there is turbulence of the dust storm; sometimes there is the serenity of a 'fading flame'. 'A blank map with no route' questions the very existence of the 'map filled borders' that divide people, waging war. When the remnant notes of the 'paradise symphony' echoes all around, 'the vagabond' disappears. We travel in a 'mad train', smell the 'last smoke', meet the 'night knight', feel the tremor in the 'silent walls', and flying on the paper wings reach the closing end. The anthology honestly records the unique blend of the scattering ideas and the deepest feelings 'from an artist's first stroke to death's last invitation'.

Our days are spent in achieving targets, meeting deadlines, shaping careers, amassing fortunes, and racing against time. Reading a book of poems may be a luxury. However, this anthology deservers some attention of the prospective readers who may find their thoughts being well expressed in the collection. The anthology may prove to be an enjoyable reading, a solace to mind or a source of deliberation. I wish *Till the last Cut is Delivered...* a sustainable success.

Jayati Chatterjee

Introduction

My journey into creative writing began accidentally through a homework exercise during my school days way back in 1998-99. Ogden Nash's work on a patient's nightmare at a dental clinic was an early inspiration before I delved into the days of Samuel Taylor Coleridge, Robert Frost, John Keats, Rudyard Kipling, P B Shelly, Alfred Lord Tennyson, William Wordsworth, W B Yeats, John Milton, William Blake, William Shakespeare, Homer, Walt Whitman, William Ernest Henley and many other classical legends.

My general aversion to authority, rules and regulations made me the wild child in the family... the black sheep! With so much bent up energy, anger and thoughts, everyday was a fight within that I had to either survive or win. The feeling of being the one who deserved and the deprived kept me on a path of self-destruction. But it was that little mundane school homework that brought me back to sane ways... I was struck by my Muse that day and it was a discovery that eventually became my immersion into the art of poetry. My escape route was thereby charted.

My Muse blessed me with that initial push and throughout my journey, I received those little nudges, nods and nags to keep trying and tire till I got my lines right. My initial joy was with rhyme, which then moved to reason, perspective, scenery, emotions... before I took the ultimate plunge to deeper territories. Mid-way, however, my focus re-directed towards seeking the approval of my Muse... I wanted to impress her than practice the art for which her intended actions were towards.

Though, a myth states that one's Muse needs an occasional prayer or offering to keep her close, get her attention, and make her happy, I did my part, a bit too far.

After many attempts in doing so, I somehow felt disconnected and unable to complete my lines or even pen a new verse. I realized on that day, that had she disappeared...deserted me. Somehow, it gave me the feeling that I was pursuing for her approval and impression rather than directing my efforts towards the sake of the art of poetry, which she had initially gifted me with. My writing journey came to a grinding halt and all of my efforts began to pile up in dust. I then moved on pursuing other avenues, seeking other adventures... but still remembering her, with mixed feelings of either me letting her down or she letting me down.

As time passed and healed our wounds, behaviours do tend to mature based on higher experiences and exposures and it was in that moment I realized that I began to miss my writing days. A passion that brought me so much joy for I was discovering myself in that journey... an art that supported me in good, bad, and ugly times. It was in that moment, I decided to revisit the art form that gave me so much freedom and the will to live. I attempted to pen a few comeback lines but this time it was without her thought in my mind. It was like reigniting a long lost love with whom you would like to reconnect without any heavy expectations.

Thrilled with this revelation and renewed with greater purpose, in mid-2015 I went back to my dusty shelves, woke up the work from the deepest slumbers, and set out on a plan to publish my anthology as an offering... to seek her out for one last time. This time it was purely to thank and acknowledge her...and yes, she did return for one last time. We shared that silent intimate moment with a smile and decided to let each other go, as a mark of respect and love. It is to her that I dedicate this offering of art... a piece of my life. I know she's around and watching over and never giving up on me... I finally understood her now.

Till the next cut is delivered, I present to you the anthology of my life's work thus far. This is the summary of my journey that I had set without mapping the destination in my mind. It has evolved with each step on paths never treaded before. If it has come this far, it is because of my love for poetry. At the end, it was totally worth it and I hope you enjoy reading it.

Vasanth Kumar J

Vaspoet83@gmail.com

www.darkknight3.blogspot.com

Acknowledgement!

To my family and friends who constantly believed in my abilities and pushed me to next level at every downward slope.

To Ms. Jayati Chatterjee, my English language teacher at school, for the early support and encouragement, without whom I couldn't have made it this far and for kindly accepting to pen a foreword to this anthology.

To Mr. Gurusundar Ram (my college senior) and his family, for allowing me to use his Personal Computer to type the poems and thereby introducing me to my first critic, the Late Chitti Sundararajan (Nonagenarian 'Manikkodi' writer and literary critic) who magnanimously gave his constructive and surprisingly, a positive review on my work.

To The Prakriti Foundation's Mr. Ranvir Shah and Ms. Meera Krish, who identified and promoted me to perform at their inaugural Poetry with Prakriti Fest & other forums for a live audience at various venues in Chennai. This also gave my first exposure as a poet to the media.

To poetess Ms. Sharanya Manivannan, who nudged me in the right direction to bring this anthology to life.

To the entire team at Partridge Publishing, having helped me realize this long cherished dream of publishing after my initial years of being rejected by several houses saying that poetry wouldn't sell.

To Mr. Amit Charles, for helping me connect with the immensely talented artist, Mr. Satya Krishna Prakash K (therearefrogs@gmail.com), who created the artwork featured in the book cover, that best represents the deeper meaning of my journey.

To all the cities, places, people, and its moments that have influenced me throughout in bringing alive the images on these pages over all these years.

To all the musicians, bands, composers & artists who have inspired and influenced me to go the distance and beyond in each piece of my work.

To all the readers across the globe who have and will come across my work in various online and offline forums and to those who cared to share their constructive views.

Finally, to the elements and to the powers that be, that brought this anthology together at the right moment with the right push and pull... in strange and magical ways. I salute you...

Cold Sale

Hazy eyes unveil, as the night begins to storm
She wanders, in her thoughts of a misty fright...
Her fading voice echoes from the windows of time
Her hands reach out...for partnering in crime.
The skies darken slowly on her whispering prayers
For another pain to cease, in silence than in violence.
Prying eyes and preying hands, that invade every space
The merciless motives that dictate her intent...

Oh, Lady in color, staring at inviting doors
Waiting in misery on pleasure scripted floors,
Papered is your soul and scarred is your gold
Wounded love of yours...is indeed so cold.
Freedom you seek from golden cages
An ugly trade of false dreams, for mighty ages
Where the nights are alive and the lights are ablaze
Passion of yours, moaned to pay-day's disgrace.

Snatched from innocence, thrown into a brave new world
She fears not death, but moans out her last words
Pain and anger, a blood-filled play on a stage of nails
Wake up lady, the lights are red, even as the sirens wail.

Seen by the eyes that do not see
Felt by the hearts that do not feel
Held by the hands that do not hold
Fueled by fever that does not feed
The deal is done and how raw it is,
I see her fade into the immortal black that is
Concealed is her choice of freedom from beneath
The unending plea of passionate screams that bequeath…

Leave her be…just let her be…
How much longer can 'He' kill 'She'?

X---X---X

Continue...

Draw me a line on the sand...
And you gave me the great divide
Hold out your hands to believe and hope
And you gave me a religious lie
Share my vengeful sorrow
And you gave the world a leaking vein
Aid me to plant a seed of joy
And you laid a minefield to lean on
Quench the thirst in my journey
And you handed me a bloody palm
Fix the wings of a falling dream
And you cut the wires to set the trigger

Wake up and open the windows dear...
Let the petrified wings fly in...
Would they? Will they? Must they?
Will you give them what you owe?
Kick the sand and repeat your sins?
Will you move to the other side, green and fair?
Will this be the script of our dear souls?

Hit the lights...crash and burn
These are favors, we must not return...

X---X---X

Decked Courage

A framed scene unveiled this flaming dream
The melting portrait of a scene...
Wondering the purpose of the dripping colors
Ashened the answers to my questions...
Was it victory that hooked my belief?
Was it defeat that sank at my feet?
Was it peace that was hard to find?
But, war it was...with an enemy lustfully blind.
Sweeping me in a raging storm of woes
A mapless destiny that posed me slow,
Kept me at peace on a throne of time
Was this a journey of subliminal crime?

Swept I was to the scene, in a flash
Draped in colors, orders and flags...
Plans lay torn on my table of sorts
As the crew closed in on its wreck
Chained was my heart in rusted steel
Bound by duty, the sword I then drew...
Rush we did with courage in our hearts
To the deck where the foes readied their arms
Rapiers and Rifles, sharpened and loaded
To silence the roars into glorified calm
The pall of smoke was the tale of the dead
For we lay as brothers on the burning deck.

With the song of the sea to carry our souls
We chorused our times in lyrical odes...
We guard now the seas after our fall
To test who passes the unending line
Immortal dreams of a mortal past
We now sail with flags half-mast...

X---X---X

Dial M for...

Hey there! It's been a while…I know.
You feel alone, so do I…but is that so?
I hope another has not fallen for you…
For you, I yearn to yield, Oh! You drifted soul.
Forgot to pay my respects, my dues
Did not count your gifts and blessings
Ingrate, cheap, and in debt I am for sure.
Do I bow to you in shame, just to lure?
Do I strip to my bones and bleed dry?
Shall I swallow to choke in the venomous air?
Must I dust my memories that rusted in time?

Script my penance…dictate my role
Direct my moves…sing my songs
Echo my screams…fill my embrace
Will you please smile…to right the wrongs?

I beg to you for I am penniless
Short of a verse to kill the fuse
Miss my reason, miss my rhyme
This is a call to you…Dear Miss Muse of mine…

X---X---X

Dust Storm

Window to my west, so is the sun
Set are the rays, wings on the run
What catches the eye is not large
Flying specks, awoken to charge.
Hovering, shimmering and swaying
Army of millions...battle-chaotic!

Just a pat beside and watch them rise
Witness in a field of rays, gravity's paradise.
May wish to float or fly away
Weightless and chainless, on any given day
Could be a dream you dare to see
Away from the madness papered in concrete

A million souls descending from the skies
Marching and singing their war cries
Like godly rains or gold dust in one's palms...
Or just the remnants of the risen phoenix

Into the realm of fading dreams
Stealing a million moments
It was a silent minute, where my world stood still...

X---X---X

Leave her be...

Scarred she is to bare bones
Drained to the dripping last drop
Dried have her tears that once flowed
Oceans are now violent, rising slow...
Bombed to bits and craters galore
Uprooted pureness that made inroads
Mined heart that shone no more
Melting white that is coming slow...
Crying skies in a venomous spat
Blood-filled soil in a vengeful act
Fading plains to a dreadful slope
Burning ground is now breaking slow...

Her burdened shoulders are aching now
Her broken bones are crumbling now
Her broken heart is pumping now
Her running veins are splitting now...
Her raped beauty will heal, but when?
Her brewing rage will cool, but why?
Her bloodshot eyes will calm, but by whom?
Her clenching fists will release, but where?

Leave her be, in her inner sanctum
Let her be, in her world of love and hate
Touch her not, for she wishes for distance
Ask her not, for she awaits her undying fate...
Penance we can, for all the sins we have done
Brace ourselves for what must be undone.
Live, with what is a clock ticking fast and blind
Else, witness this world reverse and rewind...

X---X---X

Line of Thought

A line that connects two bleak dots
Has a lot more to it, when on paper
For it defines all possible imaginations
For which, no boundaries would taper.

Fates described with palm filled sketches
Wars decided with map filled borders
People divided with historical borders
Gods decried with man-written pages

Oh how, it can break a tie, cut a lie
break the mind & lead the blind...

Visible...that have shaped history
Invisible...drawn deep in treachery
Fades away by the arms of running time
Paired to duel for partners in crime.

A surgeon to a wounded heart and a broken soul
Stitched to mend them both sans pain
The desperate connection in a journey to one's destination
From an artist's first stroke to death's last invitation.

Oh how, it can connect us all
Divide the fall & be easily drawn
On how many tales can it spawn...

X---X---X

Melodrama...

May I burn my past to ashes...and rescript the origin to suit my today
Do you see the pointless hope in me? Does it change the orbit of Mercury?

Tighten the asteroid belt a bit & speed up the storms on Jupiter
Line the stars to resemble an ape...does it impact the theory of rape?

Drop the sky and lift the oceans, side the lands and squash the beings
Tell me love, does it taste so differently? That you question Einstein's relativity?

Tell me the ending, kill the hero, break the heart, strip it bare...
Sugar my wound, moan in joy...does a bad boy scream to rip his toy?

Show me a blank map with no route, blind me, throw me to the corner
Does it satisfy your noble agenda? Oh mother mercy, pull the plug on this drama!

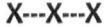

X---X---X

Run, child...

The calm breeze that caresses
Warm laughter that reminds
Exploding images and emotions
Evoke a hidden smile, which blinds.
To see you run in freedom
Is the killer of my boredom.

Defeated of illusions that we now fight
Painted with colors that throw the light

Jump and flap your wings
Run and chase the winds
Hoping that you would fly
In dew dipped gardens before they dry...

Circling ripples in the calm pond
Roaring waves in the vast oceans
Gushing winds in the dancing fields
Glittering diamonds in the velvet sky

Spreading love around
Innocence, on its basic ground
No paper, no concrete to worry
Even time waits...no rush no fuss!

All in the present, Oh! So now...
Future too, beyond and how?

Ah...that hop and the joy so mild
Run, child! This eternal world is too wild...

X---X---X

Silence the Sun...

The Pounding ounce of an eager rush
Beginning in the veins of a deepened hush,
Immortal race it is with a spoonful of hope
Mighty tales that push to the end of days.
Attempts aplenty with memorable failures
Known to many with an abridged rapier
Battle scenes won in the theatre of war
Are witnessed by the Gods, who welcome the lost.
Colored mayhem and fatigues alike
Weathered storms and shrapnel that strike
Flown by the wings that do not return
Run by the wheels that seldom turns.
Blood thirsty hounds sniff the grave
To hunt the remaining light of day
Dead men's tales that echo the night
All that remains are plaques filled names.
The ounce of courage that drove them afar
Is the love of life that brought them at par,
To a fistful of hope from a fingertip's taste
Etched in a plan that laid the sun to waste...

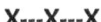

X---X---X

Smoke Dance

Defeated and deflated I once lay on my chair,
Absolutely still I was, mourning and mending a lost cause.
Foul feelings prompted me to light an incense stick
But then...I witnessed a soul-dance that shook me sick.

In all stillness, all in silence, an inch not I moved
A treat to the eye and the mind
Was a spectator to a performance, worthy for the blind.

Rising from the depths, straight and above
Motioned its ways, split its path
Poses it gave, in the masquerade
Many faces in a *Dia De Muertos* parade.

The entire pause was a lifetime in my pose,
Saw it play and sway, minus gravity
Sight of life, entwined to each other
Game they played, love in silent weather.

Tempting it was, yearning hands & yielding eyes
Seeking and calling me to take the stage.

Stunned I was till the end of the show
Dance it was, slow, slow, slow, slow...

X---X---X

Spiral Eyed

A walk in the farm with a bucketful of seeds
Skyward stare with a fistful of dreams
And then scattered...into void filled emptiness

Autumnesque paths filled in gold plated lies
Sliding across untread paths of truth filled mines
And they lead...into the star lit eyes of madness

Virtual future with more time in our hands
Oceanic depths colored by the cushioned abyss
And they speak...of stories and characters amiss

Candid photographs with silent reactions of love
Speechless solitary nomad awed by the oasis distanced
And they show...meanings of truth and lie misspelled

Galloping hooves and a tail spinning journey of planets
Spitting and gushing creatures roaring songs of tomorrow
And they slay...demons of the earth with sly filled sorrow

Ghostly veil over the moon in a black shot sky of silence
Witness the grotesque imaginations of heart pounding intentions
And they say...chivalrous and foolish are impregnable reincarnations

The waking sun now shines to rake open a tangled pair of eyes
For it ends a monstrous route-less fictional journey

Neatly dressed and decked I am, for yet another concrete battle
Gearing to die another day, living till the night calls me to bay...

X---X---X

Turbulence

If I die today, I will embrace
The approaching light or dark
Leaving behind a story, not a page
For it is not a lie, my ending on the mark...

As I fall, I stitch an open sky
Hoping to mend and mingle about
Straying in to the fields of the past
Wearing my wishes, killing my doubt.
Hoping to hold a few hands and hearts
I reach, I clench and return to myself
I console, I push, reason to let go
Born alone, just the soul to accompany me
For I am the string, I am the bow...

Play me a song that will echo
Write me a letter that will remain
Kiss me a memory that I will cherish
Battle me a war...to kill my pain.
Will you let me go, if I ask you to?
For I embrace you now, the lie to my truth...

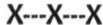

X---X---X

Deep Musings

I longed for her in aborted lands
For she left with a promise of no return
To mystical lands of mayhem and madness
Where I buried my heart, till swollen hands.

With endless journeys and abrupt endings
And leaking buckets of dreams clad drops
She tested this bard's timeless spending
With laughter in her mischievous hops.

But one day, a tear she shed, at my plight
As she watched me scathe the world across
Mourning and gnarling at my penance
I had not a drop of love, taste was of loss.

A crack in the sky, spot light, on my knees
And then…a descending soul on a landmine
Caressing and calling out my name, sublime
A savior, love it was, the name of this piece.

The ray of hope from the realm of my muse
As it descended you through from the skies
Each step worth a combing thunderous winds
As she waltzed to me with a symphony in her eyes...

Worthy seemed life now to live for, to die for
The roaring storms and the war fields of the past now pacified
Longing seem the nights for a rising sun
The wanting gaze at my love...with a loaded gun

Eyes open to thank my muse, only to see her gone
High into the skies, beyond the stars and the song
Oh my love! It was you, I forever sought,
A wait that was worth the battles I fought.

X---X---X

Early Eyes

Tender hearts beating with a pace, unmatched by aged reasoning
A heart filled innocence, joyful and inquisitive eyes without seasoning
Scenes today are shot on the streets, yearning hands and wasted tears
Skeleton legs marching for miles, heavy shoulders with sib, kith and kin

Stolen are some for treasures of tomorrow
Hidden are some, for the trade of the monsters
Snatched are their rights, left to forbidden hands
Land up in black gardens of dust and ash.
Innocent hands pulled to the sun for earning
Desperation, a source of fire, deed of the devil
A talented soul is lost, breeding acts of the veiled
With a voice of the voiceless that calls out loud
Broken are panes & cracked are mirrors...in a social world.

Hope at birth, reality to live and freedom at death...
Why do we cry at each stage, a tearful existence?
Dear child, don't beg for guns that spray mercy
Seek the fuel that rightfully fires the belly...

X---X---X

Gates

Made of steel is all that I see
Call of heaven is just a feel
Waiting in hell, I ring my bell
At the graves, a life I crave
Stone temples, solace to find
Open home, peace to bind
Prison bars, redemption time
Found in pairs, partners in crime
Wrapped in hope, chances to take
Full of gambles, for losers sake
Found in luck, a fortunate game
For the brave, a hall of fame
May be locked, may be open
But history is made, when it's broken...

X---X---X

Déjà Vu

History repeats its pages like time that had no cages…
A reflection of the past or what is to come, but a shadow
Cast into the mind, from the remnants of memory
Yearn to revisit or forget…an aching choice for ages

Who plays this scene? Was this scripted? Is it real?
A mystery, an enigma, a code or a cipher?
Ghosts of the past, seldom knock twice at your doors
But this moment from the blue, pushed me to the floors.

It exists, invisible and wicked when on song
Do the mirrors in our brain play this trick that long?

Oh yes it does…visible and ready to black the senses out of nowhere
With clues and hues, have we missed the questions to the answers?

A beauty she is at times, with a cameo so to beckon
Waiting for her to come undone, but I have not a lifetime…
She hides like the shadow below and pulls the carpet in a second

Seducing me with a pen in her arms to sign, that sly devil
Déjà Vu, she whispers… I'm yet to pay my dues!
Foolish to pen the agreement with that black soul
I paid the price with birth and death as my only role.

X---X---X

Dope Hope

Inhale...
Into caves, Out of tunnels
Swarming blue, engulfing black
Into skies, no comeback

Flying and swaying with wind under my wings
Taking me to a destination by the roll of the dice

Knocking at doors, welcomed by Titans!
Blue and gold wandering into my mind
Quenching the desires of the past,
Fulfilling the wishes of the future
Saving the state of my present
A momentary pulse of pleasure,
From the everyday chores of pressure

A wanting from the beds, to the scenes in red
A passion that strikes twice, but never promises a return...

Take me into your arms, hold me but free me
Throw me not into sorrow, for I don't want a tomorrow
Light me a candle, to flame my darkness,
With voices & visions that surround me in atmos.

Looking down, I see an orchestra playing in all madness
A song that will give me hope, a tune that will be my rope
Raising the hair on my back, a scale that will snap and attack

I am not like kith and kin that yell and scream
I am made of skin and sin, which makes me dream...

Land me into reality from these lofty stages
For I yearn not to crash and burn

Before you take me abode or push me to hell,
Help me take another drag and let my tail wag.

For there it is, my spirit that hangs high,
Hope clad, readying for that fall...
Exhale!

X---X---X

Echoed In Eternity

In a far off land, away from today's earth
I stroll on the plains…tired and hurt
Wrapped in armor & a steed beside,
A journey back home, with wounds to heal.

An ill-fated army lay behind my path
Waiting for the final blow of defeat
For I return to my lady banished in the fields
As I leave my brothers dwindling at death's feet.

As I trudge, I feel the cold wind brush my thoughts
Awakening and reminding me aloud
My brothers on red fields are blood wet
For I now step on the fields so green and set

My resting steed on the fields, where some lay resting forever
As I lie under a tree bearing fruit, waiting not for my hunger to call
Plucking from hanging gardens, I salvage what I can nearest.
Under here I sit & cherish this fruit, not of a war won, but of escape
Before it appears, there are hungry souls who await a nearing fate…

A bird then flies by to its nest, its family, to guard from me, a monster
For I see not anger in its eyes, but fear, for an end it sees by my hands.
For yes, my brothers are at the same field, fighting and defending fear
with fury
For my motherland I was born in, what I was born for and sent for.

The guilty soul awakens by heart, to wrap my gear and warn my steed
Ignoring the wounds and wiping the shame of scars I received
I turn my eyes away from home, promising only to return after the tale
is over...

Charging back from the fresh greens to the waiting reds, the galloping
paces up
Into my brother's arms, cheering them, be it defeat or the victory's
charm

My men, the wounded army take its final vow and bow, charge right
into the jaws
Where they had already been and back, with the duty we were sworn
to abide

Slay we did and so were we slain, bled till death could we not chance
anymore
Fell together but with hopes of glory written odes and monuments
beyond infinity

Will we be remembered by those who did not witness? I know not for
certain...
But we will shine my brothers, in *Elysium*, a stage at the fall of the
curtain.

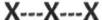

X---X---X

Fading Flames

After a hard day's journey, leaning down on your bed
The bright yellow to the last red, a path in its temporary end.

A tattoo on the horizons forehead, the eye that hides in deep waters
A star of fire and flames scorching a nightmare to the seas
The eye of an angry dragon, whose sight of fury is so undone.

You are the sword of the *Samurai*, slashing from the east, the day of war
To the west into your sheathe so long, after the bloody mess and a
deadly scar.

That fading spotlight in the blue, running out of fuel, as you move
Readying for tomorrow's colors...for now, running far, down and away.

Signaling the days end to every soul, even to the roads that bend and
lead
To the wandering mind to go to sleep, into the black where dreams
meet.

Stroking the skies that sternly claim,
For the darkness belongs to the stars, not your fame...

X---X---X

The Vagabond

White beard, torn robes, bootless and a bruised leg trudging along
Unaware of what really went wrong, an everyday sight, a lonesome song.
A zombie-like figure, in agony with each stride
A defeated warrior, who lost his final fight.

He pauses at my homely gates, regains his balance and baggage
Don't know for him, who awaits? A sign of fate and its rummage...

Muddled and wrinkled his face, mirrors, a denied grace
Rough palms and blistered feet, shelter, a denied race

No assets or treasures, no kith nor kin
But free from performance, worries and hurries

He sees faces, dreams too, so true is the picture, polluted are the streams
Some is the state, fate so sorry, sage or satan, free of role plays.

A nomad on unsettling roads, a vagabond in changing lanes
Roam he does in a hope to hold, not for stones, silver or gold.
Hungry he is for food and death, wait is long and so is the hunt
Struggle for every deep breath, moaning in pain and dreading grunts.

Wandering amidst the concrete jungle, does not bother, does not mingle
A drink or two would do him fine, candlelit or moonlit, water or wine.
Starry friends, clouding visitors, stoned bed and tiled home
Coated in dust & dirt, no cure, no hand to hold.

Wounds of time both in and out, hurt he is without a doubt
Beyond society, wise he may be, blinded we are, caged are we.

A chanced look I took, straight into those eyes, tales they had of fire and ice
A stare back, with laughter within, time stood still, lights went dim.

He spoke not, nor reacted, for his exiled silence spoke, louder than an act
He asked not a question, but reasoned, of his mission, for his treason.
He smiled and shook his head, an act that shook me hard
Felt like the fallen leaf of autumn, questioning, had I played the right card?

He resumes, with no map, corner he finds, ends to tap,
I'm back to my history lessons and the vagabond disappears forever...

X---X---X

For Whom the Bell Tolls

A soldier's tale this is, unknown, young and rank holder
Weathering the storm at his camp, trained his blood to take the martyr's stamp.

Lying in a grave so far away, unknown name, not his way
Might have lost limbs in parts...but not the spirit of his brave heart.

Gearing up for battle he was, fighting high for a lost cause
For leaders who promised a final end...only to wage a war, they sent.

Commissioned and posted in a day, forced to leave home at bay
For orders made promises hollow...as honor after death was silent sorrow.

He did promise his own, that his letter would arrive
A box of medals that shone, dead or alive.

Yes, he wanted to live, but die for his motherland
Yes, he wanted to die, but live for his motherland.

Plans were made, maps were spread, routes were checked and fences laid
Enemy shots fired and played, starry night, the smoke that swayed.

Dawn of attack, forces placed, wait was over, as time paced
Prayers were said, as hope raced, guns were loaded as rivals faced.

The snipers took down their marks, the tanks ran through the soils
Shells from the bunker took off high, but he waited in his trench and sighed.

The rain showed no mercy, pouring down the soil of hate so easy
As he sought through the falling drops, from his gear, this young corp.

Remembering his eager kith and kin, his far and distant lover, waiting in his cover.
Thinking about his dead friends, who ran into this war's bloody dead-end
Waiting for him far in heaven and watching his wait from their den.

27

The heavy droplets of rain akin to bullets giving pain
The stroke of thunder and lightning mirroring the grenades exploding
The warning fragrance closing in, from the wet soil soaking in sin
With new leaves born green, in this bloody not so clean.

The thundering command arrived from captain crazy
To charge, attack and show no mercy
Enemy lines opened bare,
Barbed wire and mines didn't care.

Every shot found its mark, hurled grenades, gone in a spark
Rapid fire, music of wars, shrieks of men, end it was
River of blood, orders and cries, deafening roars, oh...what a fight!
But our man played the gambler's wait, for the right card to set the bait

Wounded comrades came back soon
Some wished to sleep forever on the field, some prayed to live
Whispered prayers put some to rest, others rushed with songs on their lips
Many of them eighteen years, gave no damn about their fears
Some buried deep in the mud, others screamt at the sight of blood.
Fears and tears rolled down the walls, of faith and trust that called
Chain of thorns were worn within, hate and anger that roamed to sin.
Hunger and fear for food and sleep, bullets that worked in straight and deep
Ism of pain for petty gains and mercy at war is always slain...
Fly, do the bullets in no time, fences break and taken is the line
Blackouts, curfews and the sirens raid the lands of the lost

After the entire wait is over, his time came to attack and hover
Rush of blood, took a step, fists tightened adrenalin crept
Smoke and smell ruled the air, visibility, not too fair
Not sure where the enemy was, stopped and stared at his only cause.
Cries and sighs echoed out, river of death, overflowed, no doubt
Couldn't sight his rival anywhere, took his stand, ran nowhere.
No other option at sight, time to go down with one final fight.

He trod through the smoke, hunting down his enemy
Sought his compatriots in trouble, amidst the chaos
Stood his ground and took his aim, fired at will and chose to kill
Charged at the lines and strayed too far, caught at the gates and marched
to death.

Alas the marching tale halts with a tracer bullet
A crashing fable, cracked crown, bubble burst, to signal an end
With no regrets and remorse, he now had a letter to be sent
Scores of scars tearing the skin, blood of honor, spilt not thin.

Hollow and numb were his nerves, gutted was his chest
Silenced was his song of honor, as his rival saluted this valor.

Screaming a name, his last words, and a rush of memories ran through fast
Joy of his family, sigh of his love, people of his nation and the flight of
the doves.

Shots of honor fired in the air, for the martyr's band took the stage
No special grave for this lone soldier, no name on the lasting boulder.

Yes, there lies an unknown grave, of my toy soldier on the field
He did have a rifle to wield and now lies proud with a death to yield.

Lost are martyrs, unknown are some, enemy's nightmare, as they come
But my soldier now lives, in the company of souls that dwell in eternity...

X---X---X

Last Smoke

Killer pipe tunneling from dark to light
Strike of the match to burn it bright
Spray paint the sky in a mad want for freedom
Parched lips wanting a pull to kill the boredom
Measured inhale for a pale pleasure
Emotional release through a scarred fissure
Ceases pain, extending lone memories
A slithering friend, foe in amber emeries

An unnoticed sin laced with ghostly spirits
A hollow promise seeking the ghastly souls
A smooth touch to a crash landing zone
A gambler's roll to a psychopath's control
A trooper's zone, a veil of the unseen agenda
A racer's course, the shroud of an owner's vendetta
A writer's block, the ending of a long awaited novel
A vendor's wait, the purpose of the enterprising grovel
A choker without diamonds, with fingers of death
A lullaby without words, with an unending story
A butcher without meat, with a knife on bright sparks
A death without hope, with fading life in a pool of sharks

Hero's fear, villain's pride
Lover's tear, artist's stride
Shakespeare's Lear, Bonnie's Clyde
God's never near, Devil's always aside
To witness the wandering you on a high, lost and found
The curtained blue, hanging and oscillating low and around
Forever the styles of the enchantress wait till the end, Dear Miss...
Smile my Love, it's an invitation to partake in death's last kiss.

X---X---X

Mad Train

I journey in lands never seen before
Wheels on tracks that dictate my destination
The mile long worm chugging through the black smoke
With a hooting loco, roaring its song
Creaky goods and freaky passengers on its load
From this very world and afar from another.

Tearing through dancing narrow bridges
Upon screaming rivers calling and clawing its ways up
Caving through blackened tunnels, waiting for the light
Pacing under the staring and pale blue sky
Coloring them in shades, dark and dry
Creaturely clouds shape shifting and alive
Shattered stars, mapping my journey wild.

The racing wheels took its toll
Pushing and pulling around
Belting the madness from its tail
Into my head, now in a trance.

The halt finally came at an insane edge
With a lonely station that showed no sign
All the characters now visible from my window
In sanity's motion, walking death row.

Unleashed both from the gates of heaven
And released from the broken cages of hell
Staring at my window, calling me out they were
A platform that now seemed their haven.

Vasanth Kumar J

My killing thirst pushed me out the door
To quench my parching soul, my wanting hands
Exit I did watching the suspicious signal
Waiting for it to cheat my wandering eyes.

As I have my fill, now overflowing with fear
The stationary monster sends its cue...
In a pace that couldn't be caught by aged minds
The desperate running feet raced like a child

It all unveiled like a perfect plan
To leave me behind in that nameless station
But I ran till the end of the world,
Leaping to reach out to the door
Threading myself to the handle

I then see a claw creep out of the blue
Faceless, with a motive so clueless
I cling on to the arm, hoping for help
But then the monster halts at the tallest bridge
Right over a hungry river raging below, no escape route
The claw turns to sand, disappearing into oblivion
Letting me off with a wild laughter in the winds
The fall was long, gravity absent in its evil duty,
The murky monster above, mocking as it lurks
The infinity barrier below, wakes me to go to work...

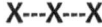

X---X---X

Night Knight

Onset of the deep dark black, most are off, tucked in their sack
There are wings that rule the sky, break the silence, with a kill so high.

With the faded blue now so gone, a pitch black field is now on song
Still of the night now is broken…hunters of the night, gates are open.

Flapping hard and screaming loud, never a shadow under the cloud
Roaming in the age old loneliness and often scare in stillness.

A hunt for blood, game begins, no armor, sword or shield
Weapons of choice, wings and fangs…sky wide open battlefield

Resting when the fire is up, rushing under the stars, though blind
For this winged warrior's piece of mind, peace is not hard to find

Cold when hot, it befriends the stars that shine so high
Enemy of the day, a comrade of the night…

Like the ghosts of time running wild and free
They fester like the devil in you and me…

X---X---X

Paradise Symphony

Creators of magical scenes for all, right from the invasions to the fall
From the blackening to the new blue, the outbursts that leave no trace
or clue

Howling chords pull the ears, scare and chill ones fear
That dark onset and the gathering, witnessing and whistling

All in black, with their instruments, ready to pour in their moments
Of deep pleasures and dark passions to flood the mind...empty and set.

When the landfall scripts the ground, a tale is written in sound
Lyrical ballads are all I hear, a heavenly ballet is what I see.

Strings of genius cut the skies with all the scales and melodies
The riff and rage on the stage scare and stare to turn the conductor's pages

Lightning the souls with fire and the ice, where submission is generally wise
Receiving the ovation just to realize, hidden desires need to capsize.

Lastly for that finishing stroke, where every emotion taunts a choke,
The cleared stage now haunts after a stormy finale, echoing the remnant
notes...

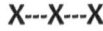

X---X---X

Pirate, I Am...

Pirate I am, of the magnificent seas, stealing riches and looting hearts
Fluttering flags and sounding horns, ship of ours, The Lady of Thorns.

Sailing with the winds, against the waters, from dawn to the blackest of dusk
In starry nights with a heavenly map, a route is never fixed with certain luck.

Times have filled on death like stillness, dancing storms with a shaking fate
Howling winds, cutting hate, warning cracks, sinking hopes.

Stolen fortunes, in our pockets, laughter and tears, from the lockets
Slaves and masters, on the docks, friend and foe, keys and locks.

Guns and swords, execution time, thieves and outlaws, escaping crime
Onto my ship, is that crew on the knife, who sail an adventure worth a dime

Behind the wheel, I set my sights, directions to a wonder territory
Another port to halt and break, eat and drink, with women in merry.

Ghostly faces, haunt the nights, on the decks with their gnawing whips
and claws
We set to sail with all booty's breadth, with penalties of death for
outrunning the law

Capturing rivals along our way, blood for blood, on traitor's day
Cannons and gun powder fill the air, the smell of victory, the cigar's flair.

Tales of us with ghosts and curses, filling our hearts and our purses
King of the seas, servants of our will, we are outlaws, on a pill.

Music of the sailor, merry and joy, sorrow hates us, death welcomes us
Bread and wine, fills our senses, gold and silver, keeps us alive.

Sights of sea creatures below the blue, leviathans sailing under our sights
Calls of whales, song of the sea, serpents and dragons, myths to believe.

Souls of time, fly around our sails, talking to sailors, telling them tales
Protecting us from the omens, guiding us to the light from the dark.

Months on water, on our decks, with brothers watching from the nest
Sail is high, tide not far, into the sunset, way beyond par.

No home, no belonging, no love, no land, just me arms of the sea, hold me, O Mother!
For I seek not the maidens, nor the barren sand, for we are the maverick brigands.

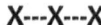

X---X---X

Pushed to hell!

Bells have rung, not in peace
Loud in pain, down on your knees
Hidden tears are on the rampage
History has added another page.

Walls around close in
Birth is a mistake, the sin within
To live this world, in chains
Arrest of tears and the resting chin.

Pushed from the gardens to the knife
With hidden thorns and waiting pits
A shattered home and a shared heart
A hit too hard that tears dreams apart

False smile to fool the eye, nice words mince and sigh
Gifts to welcome and to greet, a push for someone else's greed.

Opened your heart to just a few, I was there, so were you
Powerless and helpless in favor but the toast of the family's only flavor.

End of dreams that mystified
Nightmares begun, crucified
Pushed are the doors, open wide
So were you, devil had to decide.
Smoke within, heart that burnt
Tears hidden, flooded eyes hurt
Wings cut, freedom in a cage
View blocked, anger and rage.

Music to some, pain to you, bond to some but not to you
Holy chain around, a noose to you...the God of fire to witness you.

Into the flames, with the smoke, deep into waters and ready to choke
Falling hits harder than rage, you've tripped too far and now's the chase.

Hope you float in murky waters, fight the way out of this mutiny
Set an example to other daughters, bring shame this fallen society

May you walk around the fire no more, stride through the fire no more
May this be a life worth dying for, by re-writing the ancient lore...

X---X---X

Sakhi!

Tale it is, unraveled in a dream,
Two hearts in union, beating fast
But an end, turning the heat at last.

A fine still night, hoping to see a tale unfurl
All I see is an epic saga to tell,
Starring me and a character from hell.

She was a blinding beauty, rising from the treasures
In all temptations, arrowed my heart, blinded my eye
The ride began and reality waved goodbye.

Hypnotic eyes, river raging hair, that devilish smile with kisses to share
Call of cupid, echoes of love at first sight, blinded from above.

Moments we had much too close, smelt a fish but gave her the rose
Entrapped in her lasso so long, her noose was on song.

Took me to lands mirroring paradise, in her efforts to entice
Hummed in duet all set to tune, unaware I was above her dune.

And finally to the gates of her abode, she let loose the ghosts, awoken
Where the gates of hell were ripped and broken

Songs became screams, loud and proud, surrounding me in her majestic
shroud.
All waiting with patience tested, ready to pounce, on a soul so vested
Gullible and healthy to join her legion...I was the only human in that region.

A change of colors and in shape, all in robes, ready to rape.
Doomsday storm forming over my head, chants pouring for readying
the stew

Bolted doors and fallen floors, the devil's orchestra began its roar
With all the courage I mustered, I conveyed my lines to her...

Reminded her of our love lore, all the hugs, kisses and many more
All the rides, songs and skies we'd soared, fights for and against the world

Silence erupted in the assembly, shattering her roar
For she ordered a halt...temporary.

Chance she gave me, memories gave her fury.
I was now the master of my dream, rising from my fall

Knowing I was taken over, I ordered the troops of my state.
Charging with their symbols and signs with weapons of choice to charge and kill

Scene of war, amidst it...she stood still, staring at me and our memories
Her scream of anguish shattering the panes of her dome she built for me...
A swift invasion ensued...left she was, stranded and found guilty.
Captured she was, by my marching saints, placed in a coffin of chills and pains

She made her move, her only choice, reappeared as her true self, back as my love
Crying my name, fake tears, loud promises, hollow within

My ignorance gave her pain and fears, defining her doom
As we ordered the end of the act, the end was on her soon...

Through the creaking coffin doors, she finally saw her antics, now beyond reach
Her seduction once hard to breach, was her punishment, six feet deep.

I awake, wilting profusely, for my nightmare has finally ceased,
Realizing the episode was over, a fantasy turning bad for this lover.

Recalled the drama that ended close, mighty moments, risky but lucky...
Couldn't ask her name, that black rose...what hell! I named her...Sakhi!

X---X---X

The Shadow Boxer

That dancing black on the wall
Ready to strike at the bell's call
Your true figure beating the air
Your rival in the firing line, does not care.
Acting akin a moving mirror
Reflecting instincts, spreading terror
Swift, fast, heavy or light
Preparing to fight for that longing spotlight.
Giving this silent champion one last chance
To practice again with his unique dance
Train him to be the best, to go as far
Give his enemy, one lasting scar.
You may knock out your bloody sins
Fight like your life depended on it
Care not for those who pray and hum...
For now, your bout is waiting, come undone...

X---X---X

Silent Walls

Abandoned sand invaded the floor
Crack on the wall…that stench in the air
Emptiness and hollow till the door
Was a tale, fair and square.
Broken windows, dusty panes
Black throughout, past of pains
All the pages, tattered and torn
Demolition duty, hunt to borne.

A glance gives a picture of years filled with silence
Dark and deep, a feature…probability of desperate violence
Or memories, tender…a happy ending with tragic bends

Sand and paper, trashes and ashes, bricks and rods in dust or rotten
Glass or wood to pierce and scathe, light of hope to faded scrap.

Home to the souls for heaven and hell, residing to ring the hanging bell
Home to silence that softly kills, echoing the calls that keep you still.
Home to legs, tails and eyes, in remains and the rubbles of time
All in rust and no price a dime, looked like chance's ultimate crime.

Rains now fill the empty spaces
The sunlit roof and the fall to the dusty floors
Idle is the mind at the devil's workshop
So is this home, whose haunting will not stop…

X---X---X

Sketches in the Sky

Chameleon traits that make eyes wait
To observe and find living sketches hiding
Hidden paintings that come to life, silent invasions on the knife
Witness a saga or a bout, without a doubt
From the early blue, to the late black
Shades and hues, a moody pallet painted you...
From the gold shimmer of torn carpets, to the fusion in colorful shrouds
You may see the gleaming creatures, floating scary and awry
That deceptive pale to the deafening dark, the fiery crimson and raging red
To the blips and blinks, an old movie with unknown names
Conquering color when it pours, dull and pale when the curtain lowers
Never falling from its grace, watching over the lands with not one face
Different strokes in their grace, dame like twists & twirls, curls & curves
Traveling smoke after flames, ash filled dreams that lures
Roaming beasts in the sky, murky faces trying to cry
Angry dragons breathing fire, people fighting for desire
Slashing swords piercing through, rubble in the field and castles too
Ruined forts, mythical figures, sparks flying and looking eager
Ancient birds that flock in formation,
Mighty ships that dock in temptation
Roaring tigers, purring cats, wolves in packs
Eagles that soar, to sharks beyond the shore
Moving monuments, coffins in the pall
Chariots in time, to the bandits in crime.

They too have stories to tell...of kings and queens and ringing bells
Marching soldiers fighting in time, jesters and clowns with laughter a dime
The galloping knight in shining armor, the general and his men, bowing in honor
The sky is enough to dream about, infinite sketches to wipe your doubt
Watch it sketch a tale or two, else choose your script with a heroic hue

X---X---X

Soul Driver

Scene in the city, me in black and on duty, the devil is back
Search is on, sunrise it is, till the sunset's kiss.

Echoes in the wind calling a name
Calling me, for a dangerous game
For time it was, for the kill, what a moment of thrill!

I play a new role, to drive away the black soul
From the depths of invaded purity
Dark and silent working with anxiety
Signs and chants, weapons of choice
Fear and hope, a calling voice
From the heart of innocent
Held by the claws of madness.

Skies turned red to my searching eye, running clouds fighting fire and ice
Struggling and gasping for a release, I fight the demons that need to unleash.
The possessed girl kept to the corner, crying her heart out to me, the savior
I rush to her feet, holding her close, with trust and belief for the devil
she chose.

She holds on to her only respite, seeking help, pain despite
I close my eyes, open my heart, convince to the gods to play their part.

Escape it is…for the blackest deed, run it does, releasing itself from greed
From the girl's sanctum, its haunted home, the softest target, circling
it's dome.

But the chase had only just begun…for the spirit was now on the run
Flying from each wall to open doors, another victim down on the floors.

This time, it possessed a stronger youth…smart choice I felt, but motive not
Violent encounter it was for sure, a tough rival that denied the cure.

Finally held him down to the floor,
Nailing him, with a holy folklore
Ready for a final fatal blow he was
Until I saw another coin toss.

Wicked wings spread and threw me away, a loud scream that drew me
insane
Bloodshot eyes in a silent sight, gave me a chase and worth the fight.

Jumping across roofs, climbing walls, it laughed and kept running its course
Into the action with a mortal fall, I failed to chain it to sanity's hall.

It stopped few yards away and turned…to see me fail in my lonely chase
An evil smile flashing on its face…familiar scene, signaling for another
immortal race…

X---X---X

Bad To The Bone

Two hidden horns, one long tail
Loud wicked laugh, scent of the trail
Hands that teach, legs out of reach
Laws to breach, more to preach
Work at night, sleep at day
Dark is bright, dare I say
Snap of fingers, rush of maids
Blink of an eye, trades that fade
Dressed in white, black is the heart
Guns are many, bullets are sharp
Bag of drugs and street fight knives
Rush for gold, an evil mind strives.
Talk of gold, touch of death
Fast lane life, walk of panache
Tricks under sleeves, living dying breath
Dust to dust, ash to ash
Eyes on you, law hunting you
Murky lair, gangster's paradise
Cash in plenty, dimes anew
Time ticks fast, roll of the dice
Life is yours, death is mine
Tale of his, epic in a line...

X---X---X

Sky Reel

Fascination is at its peak, as stars in the night so do speak
Of tales and myths so glorious…of maps and fads so adventurous.

Search for them in oblivion, feel them guide above and fall in
To sleep under those lights, fixed on the far back wall
Witness each one shine bright and no one to fight and fall,
See them exhibit their shades…of brightness in darkness that fades
From the pole stuck in its place, to the nomads at light years grace.

Connect the dots for shapes of myths and legends draped in black
Tales of forgotten lore, filled with reasons and lessons to back.
Feel them travel on their magic carpets, play the fool like fireflies
A lonesome heart shining, a team winning or losing in its strides…

Link them all up and see nations amongst the scars
Create a figure or a character, pen down your creed or charter.
Existing constellations live on, create yours, name one, it isn't a crime.

Their absence may hurt a lot, when they hide behind the storms
Or trotting clouds for a while, or when the bright solar ball dawns.
When conquered by the mists, veil amongst the silent shroud
Peeping from the gaps and holes, for that glimpse…the wait of woes.

Every poet's apt dream, a nomad's mighty scene,
Lover's speechless romance, proposal ring's diamond,
Pearls in the shadows, fallen from sore hands coarsened by time

Don't they see us grow? Witnessing what time does?
A spotlight, foe or lover…making dreams to hover?
Shattered glassy shards, crystal like in its class
Thorns in the dark soil, warning not to foil.

Filled in a dark mine, when discovered, just shine...
Whichever king made a mark, troop or truce or ally
Soldiers to the moon, serving for his cause, their positions, war it was.
A true friend to the navigator lost in time in the seas of no return.

They may be far, far away, light the dark, they say
Blink or stare hard and fast, as each death and birth has a cast.

With the unexplored galaxy still waiting for our dreams that are negating
For some may be the pinnacle, if not, better ask the oracle.

Yes, fascination is at a peak, when they giggle, dialogue and peek
For they are witness to tales so glorious...creator of courses for adventures.

You may miss them, when you need them at your helm
They may miss you too...hey, for they need gazers too!

X---X---X

Paper Wings

Wish I had the wings to fly
Strings attached to feel the cry
Float in the skies, just to be free
Flying with paper wings to flee.

I'm flying with fatal fantasies in my hands
Paper wings, loose strings, high above the lands

Oh...my pilot, down below
With just a string to keep my control
When the winds may die or reveal
Warn us, the sky is to steal.

Gusty winds with souls on the move, other friends get in the groove
Fight for the sky, war is on, war of strings, challenges are coy and con.

May be long, may take me far
Pull me closer, horizons at par
Entangled hopes, now is the chance
Hold me tight, for I am in trance.

West is where lies my only hope, for the dark is scary to cope
Hope to decide soon to kill or get killed, for my last song is in tune.

I may sleep forever before I see the stars
Or wake up to see tomorrow's scars
Wish to roam free where the winds take me
Another hand, fresh strings, another spree.

Torn and cut by other fangs
May not have a life or a chance
Oh...these wars, loose in my dance
That dream of cloud nine, with my lance.

Could have been high or below, for my dreams are not slow
A free bird always whispers to the winds, take me...for I am the shadow!

X---X---X

Rewind

Dreaded death... birth of life
Lost love...regained and revived
Lost enemies...cherished rivalry
Once friends...first strangers
Trigger shots...returning bullets
Gains earned...turned to losses
Losses displayed...churned to gains
Chances received...pleas for grants
Roll of the dice...back to the hands
Hunt for survival...nullified chase
Crimes galore... scripting one's motive
Lifestyle gadgets ...to breaking sweat
Glorious planes...hung in the hangars
Bulking ships...designing to the docks
Striking towers...foundation of brick and sand
Snaking trains...pushing to walking journeys
Social networks...glad for conversations
Modern society...back to civilization
Many religions...reaching one god
Superstition...applying common sense
Mixed race...return to identity
Raging rivers...freezing to ice
Pouring rains...evaporation to the sky
Purging fires...plugging back to the sparks

Vasanth Kumar J

Live music…originating tribal thumps
Performance drama…living in reality
Blooming flora wrapped back in buds
Lurching fauna absorbed to the womb
Cover of trees rooting beneath the earth
Big to small, small to big
Man came early, undone with leaf and twig
If those garden gates were bolted and bound
Adam redesigned, drawing board with light and sound
Eve could have refused that forbidden bite…
Evolution's powers that be, might was always right…

X---X---X

Chained To Pain

Cuts you through, pierces hard
Bloody hell, one wrong card
Scream within, tears are out
Rips your bones, live a doubt
Cuts like ice, makes you shiver
Jump in the fire, drown in the river
Fall too hard, numb you feel
Silence kills, grave is the deal.
Pitch dark is all around you
Empty heart, something is due
Parting ways, force or fault
Running fury, a distant halt.
Neglect phase, wrong is the time
Wishes fade, forced are your crime
Losing hope, wait at the gates
Pressure mounts, in dire straits.
Something chews, gnaws you full
Handing lose ropes and chains to pull
Sleepless nights that haunt forever
Seeks and chooses to hunt your lover...

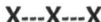

X---X---X

Vasanth Kumar J

Dark Side Of The Moon

Nothing is what it seems to be...one side exhibition on a spree
With a journey down the deep shall reveal and make crawl-creep.

Where one part of the story is said, of dragons that hid under the bed
Where a masquerade takes place...fooling the eye in all its grace.

Where the mirror scares and plays a game unveiling all the dark names
Unfolding all the horrors of time, nailing the coffin of an empty crime.

To every head, a longer tail and with every hunt, a lasting trail
War between the black and white, battling in grey lands with ones might.

Where every man has his colors, but the shadows show only black
In dreams with all fervor, carrying broken wishes and roaming forever.

In seas that may seem silent, down below, is a war so violent
Where the stars above shine so bright, a gas ball flames the fight.

Every flower does pull a nose...when the bee's yard is just close
For every rose guarded by thorns, one calm bull with two mighty horns.

When winds can soothe and uproot, earth to support and ploy
When waters can purify and nullify, flames to warm and destroy.

Where work was for money, not a shade of value, so phony
Witnessing lives drift so far away, in others arms that trick and play.

Where love lies in between the lines, shines the unseen motives that rhymes
So deeply hidden in sarcasm are dark, trivial statements and conspiracies
that bark.

Where happiness comes with sadness, where gains have their shares
of losses
With every birth, life or death, every hero fights a villain's mad cause.

For the very god, a devil in every prayer, to every calm in a silent peril
The unseen story of the blue moon, is the face I'd like to see soon...

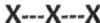

X---X---X

Kudos

That usual cry of war
Back benchers, full of sign and scar
Smiling at the enemy down the line
Right in front, those ranked to shine.
Silent jokes spreading fast
Giggles in genes, signs of the past
Chatting and planning with deft secrecy
Search or study, play is in the scene.
Passing looks and signs to their mates
Silent trap who fall for the baits
Ink fights reign, chalk wars seen
Collar catching, rioting wild, wrestling by the lean
Knocked out is the referee, in comes the dean
Kneeling till it reaches high noon
Authority reaching to hand us our doom.
A shower of abuse, in a mad bloody pool.
Dismiss, punish, whatever it may,
Will stop us not, on any given day
Whatever breeds or rowdies we are
We define an age that tear norms apart...

X---X---X

Early Angel

Born she was, only daughter
mother's pride, gave no quarter
realms of a bloody war, civil it was, way beyond par.

Witnessing many a massacre, hearing all their screams
Feeling the vibration of the falling shells
Arrested she was, by the curfew's calling bells.

She strode with tears, filling an ocean...into red waters flowing with emotion
With bodies washed on every shore
She had never witnessed a war before.

Marching troops, filling the roads...tanks and vans, to clear the mobs
running feet and beating hearts
run she does, home is far.

In all the hunger and the thirst, she slept in the dark, far from light
the light of fire and shadows of smoke
for days had passed, lost in the fight.

Ring of bell, end of school
open gate, walk to home
friend and foe in all a laughter
but tide is turned for this daughter.

A sudden silence moored on the scene
A raging storm to roar and pour
Standing still in a silent doubt
She saw the mob scream and shout.

Sirens and alarms, deafening her
As her trembling feet refused to move
hope of home now fading fast
Fear gripped her good, moments to last.

Molotov cocktails akin to preying hawks
The ghostly smoke, hovering to choke
Raging flames, hungry for ashes
Kept this little angel, on the run.

The troops now invaded the streets
So did the fears, imprisoned many a heart
Instant death, if they questioned that immortal seat
Justice served once the silk had been torn apart.

Run she did, on those burning roads
Tender feet pierced by hatred
Innocent face blackened by smoke
A bleeding angel, draped in red

Shelter she found around the corner, away from the erupting hell on earth
silence and hunger, put her to sleep
Shutting her eyes, hoping for a dream.

The empty playground now filled with as many angels from heaven
Where love and joy was never billed
Where birds would fly till even.

Filling colors into her wanting mind, guiding her to a beautiful day
knowing not what reality could blind
the sights of a lonely highway.

The piggy back ride on her grandpa's back, hugs and kisses of her mother...beautiful
The broad shoulders of her working father...powerful
Her smile in a disturbed sleep...blissful.

Then someone comes by, as she refuses to leave those wings so pure white
Waking her eyes to open and sight
Granting a chance, to spot the light.

A voice, a hand, the face...mother like! Calling her, gently holding her
That wait, for her arrival
Moment in her dreams, so eternal.

Thinking it was her, opened her locked and bolted eyes
She fades into darkness, stepping back to the bloody reality, out of her
gardens...
The search for that motherly voice was finally on...out in reality's lawn.

Army on the east, mob on the west
armed and ready, fences put to the test
the final effort, to bring an end
this battle at the devil's bend.

Center stage, emerges a searching voice
A mother's call for her lost child
A hunt in the wild fields like scene
Calling out a name, her only hope.

Ordered she is...back off for safety
But a refusal thunders back in vicinity
A final cry of despair is out
the angel eyes open, to clear her doubt.

A moment of silence, to define it all
that death wouldn't stop her last call
The call of a desperate mother,
Her scampering feet, delays the violence.

Tracing the echoes, she ran with remaining life
trembling and tumbling feet
rampaging tears pouring in joy and pain
Felt like heaven was back again.

Back in the arms of her mother
End of a search for them both
A signal of hope for many another
Amidst the staring war, of lost brothers.

Until one trembling finger tripped the trigger
And silenced the cracking vocals, weeping eyes
The fall was silent, lasting was the hug
Drama of the dead are scripted with tragedies

Unaware, she carries her away from the madness
as promised, into her favorite playground
Far away from the mortal days
Into eternal love and immortal ways.

But down below, she's lost her voice
In the shock at what lay in her arms
Breathless and lifeless, fatal stroke
A mother's emotions, with bloody palms.

Bloodshot eyes, staring at death in silence
Disbelief and anger, invading her heart
Scream she did, before the words that choked
She would then speak and curse the world.

"What if she was your blood?
What if I was your mother?
Why kill butterflies with bullets when even traps can't catch their colors?

You fill this land with unforgivable sin and think of winning this civil war?
Why act like gods, when you are mortal? Can you give back life with
your force?
Does it power you to script the fate of battles? Can you change this course?

With my blood wasted on this land, I beg this assault to halt…
Else the curse of a mother's sorrow, is the last thing you'll want to hear
Let not early angels crowd the heavens…"

The hell bound troops fell frozen and silent at their acts so violent
Death stood still, in all devotion…reality now, gave light to blinded eyes

Saw the colors they used to fill the streets, staring at their own bloodied hands
they begged for forgiveness, on merciless lands.

None moved a step, dare they...but a step behind, all in guilt
For the demons now were silenced and driven away to rot in filth.

A mother's silent sorrow would now prevail...an invisible curse, without fail
A child's silent cry would now haunt empty streets and mind's violent jail.

Only the good die young, for earthy mortals live short
Witness the skies crack open to those...the powers that chose
Saving the worthy to whom hell was a touch too close...

X---X---X

Keep Smiling

Win or lose
Break or make
Meet or leave
Sing or silence
Play or rest
Try or tire
Scream or whisper
Love or hate
Speak or listen
Fight or settle
Serve or served
Sleep or awake
Laugh or cry
Read or write
Open or close
Run or stay
See or blind
Create or destroy
Sketch or color
Work or fired
Drink or eat
Fly or sail

Discover or hide
Explore or stay
Share or keep
Hold or held
Pray or believe
Strive or relax
Struggle or laze
Enter or leave
Welcome or welcomed
Play or played
Sway or swayed
Hope or be hoped upon
Keep smiling on and on and on...

X---X---X

Skin Strike

I kissed the valley of death
Scent of the dew filling my senses
Walked through the village of shadows
The reason for many a war
In open and tempting meadows.
Twin peaks with tombs atop
Holding the holiest of waters
Feeding the hunger of roaming souls
Quenching the thirst of parched humanity.
Calling and screaming the serving names
Playing and fondling with the mind games
Dicey to court, tricky to hold
Dare it is, take it or not.
Violent minds prey from all directions
Crouching powers from every dimension
Wrestling for positions in common grounds
Bloody it is on first rounds.
Race of emotions, rush of blood
Hold of grip, fold and flip
Tower of glory, standing tall
Heaven or hell, one night's call.
Dawn of dusk, blow of horn
End of heat, end of song
Wet grounds, breathless in sweat
Angels and demons settle the debt.
The bitter sweet moon fades away into silence and time,
Within moments of passing of the unholy storm and struggle
The wave that swept blood and bones afloat and afoot
Was the music that made us sway, but still gave us the boot!

X---X---X

The Unsung

Tanned skin that sow the soils
Feed hunger that always grows
Blistered heels that plough the fields
With tired eyes waiting for the rains
Beating hearts pray at the doors
Muscled hands that lay the bricks
Bare feet that tile the floors
Skilled fingers that wire the walls
Soiled feet that clear the pipes
With tired eyes closing to the night song
Sleepless hearts that take to the highways
Burdened shoulders that load the wheels
Seated hopes dare to dream of a halt
Thankless souls on vigil at the borders
Sleepless spirits give others a snore
Courageous hearts guard long laid fences
Singing to their homes about lonely lives

Homeless are some, blessed by the skies
Deprived are some, bled by the earth
Downed are some, dressed by freedom
Alone are some, wet by the tears
When do we reach out to them?
When do we answer their calls?
Do we, when our stomachs are full?
Do we, when our muscles pull?
At least say hello (lest the handshake)
At least say goodbye (lest the wave)
If not, a simple apology (long due),
Then a quick appreciation (still pending)

Lend not your fortune...lend not your home
Share a minute with those who call to you
Nameless are many, lost are plenty
Give them a hand or a shoulder, walk their road

Life ends not with the luggage, but just the ticket in hand
Life ends not with the accumulated, but with empty bags
Miss not the journey, miss not the colors that paint a story
Miss not the people, miss not their souls, draped in gritty glory...

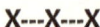

X---X---X

Unseen Nation

'47, born again
End of struggle, end of pain
New minister, new ministry
Independent gain.
Vote for me, vote for you
Democracy, black and blue
Mob & riots, bomb & blasts
Cloud of war, smoke of castes
Firing on borders, operation & missions
Emergency galore & silent curfews
Conspiracy and the hue
Legacy families, pocket filled hypocrisy
Don deals, landing controversy
Empire east, slum west
Religion, skin trade
Sati, animal sacrifice
Fasting cause, stunt a fight
Child marriage to entice
States split, mapping region
Quota discrimination
Brute kill, hit & run
Assassination, gang rapes
Lotus Eater, slapping palms
Rocket deals, arms pacts
Bank accounts, black money
Plug points, hard drives
Navy deals, sanctions act
Sandalwood, blood for good
Drying water table, playing under table
Government policy, vision 2020 unstable
Salary hikes, wage boards
Born free, still in cages
Fashion cost, torn for a cause
Tension profits, mounting losses

Brand war, tongue in cheek
Ad craze, disposition
Burning pockets, hole so deep
Rapid change, less to start
Stock market, bulls & bears
Flora & fauna, malls & market
Movie hall, Smart phone
Temple treasures & ruined forts
Jammed stations & lonely ports
Light in villages & road to towns
Wrap *Dhoti* & silky gowns
World Bank, looming debt
Economy, slow bet
FDI pull, FOREX push
Balance Sheets, Suspense Accounts
Unbalanced justice, innocents are suspect
Glass towers, clay roofs
B–Schools, unemployment
Cricket, Bollywood
IT Sector, Make in India
Common man, Robin Hood
Villains & heroes
Numbers & zeroes
Northie, Southie
Westie, Eastie
All in one, all so fun
My nation...an unseen passion

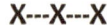

X---X---X

Smoke On The Water

Two strangers met, no more they were
Friends they became, thick in time
Two bloods, two souls, one they were
No doubt…partners in crime.
Interests they shared, same in tastes
Both were soldiers, in their ranks
Borders they broke, rivalry a waste
Peace they hunted, far from tanks.
Both were away from their nations
Traveling they were in foreign lands
Explored new truths and other stations
Knowing soon death would glance.
Laughter they shared, jokes they cracked
Sorrow they borrowed, tears they had
Drink and a cigar, a soon stormy weather.
Call from camp, much too soon
Looked like trouble had just begun
Packed their bags, ready to leave
Both parted ways, memories to run.
A promise they made before departure
That this rendezvous would happen again
Knowing not what future to capture
Heading for war, both were in.

Reported to their camps, in the field
Blue was one, Crimson, the other
Rivals they were, river at stake
Invisible hate, visible brother.
Cannons placed, fences embraced
Belts worn to set the tone
Dynamites fixed, feelings mixed
Guns were ready, heavens they kissed.

Blue, due east of the river
Crimson, lay to the west
Face to face with honor and pride
To color the water in war's ride.

Command's charge, loud and clear
Rush of adrenalin, dear oh dear
First steps became last to glory
Others marched in sands with fury.
Bullets cutting the winds past through
Others found their mark, painful hue
Escaped some, hurt were others
Stuck in the middle, retreat was close.
The waters now filled to the core
Of dream filled corpses and lifeless yearning limbs
Soaked in blood of others and their own
Brothers in arms, no mercy shown.
The might of the Blue, shocked the enemy
The swift of the Crimson, stunned the rival
Both fought with courage for honor
Glory and destiny, soon to bother.

The halt of the war, came not soon
Bloody o' battle, hard to fine tune
Smoke of the guns took its stage
Engulfing the waters in heavens rage.

Emerged our heroes from either side
From the fresh deaths of each soil
Called out for survivors, where silence plied
Clearing the waters, where they had toiled.

In anger and anguish they screamed so loud
Shattered the silence, a miserable shroud
Both heard each other loud and clear
Plot unfolds as they spoke, no fears.

Crimson Soldier in a cry of anger
Echoed back a voice so deafening
A reply that stunned both apiece, to wonder
Fate sealed, no chance to surrender.
"I have a bullet left...Blue devil
for we meet in this silence, ghostly smoke
Unable to sight you, but I care not
For my aim is clear, miss I will not"

Replied "Oh Crimson warrior...unseen to me
Reminds me of a voice, not long ago
Who spoke of bravery and courage so true
So here I am, let's give it the go.
Bullet apiece we both have
Let the gods meet and decide
Let us fire through the smoke, not hide
For one death shall define the side."

Said he "I hear you brave one...
Take our mark, keep our word
Close my eyes, hear my heartbeat
Duel it is, not miles apart."

Crimson echoes..."aim I have taken Blue devil
For I am the Crimson for sure
Take your aim and count to three
For our ends shall be so pure."

Silence lasted after these words
Beats that raced, felt was near
Trusted the smoke and the enemy beyond
Heavenly fools, brotherly bond.
Breath they took, deep it was
Looked like now death had its cause
Trigger so ready, moments closed by
Smoke so set, waters waited.

End of count, cry of 'Now'
Silence shattered and battered somehow
Cutting metal through smoke that pierced
Cry of pain...the end scripted fierce.

Both fell with a splash so hard
As both played the winning card
Both won, none lost afar
Settlement drawn, end of war.

Waters were shared as a condition
Of the treaty so signed, no concession
But, it took a battle to find
A solution existing, just to bind.

Comrade's promise, duly kept
Their rendezvous happened again
Embracing joy and igniting freedom
A bloody reunion, never again

The skies welcomed by the keepers above
Gates opened for the bravest of souls
No one in uniform or ordinance wrapped for rhyme
Brothers met, reunited, rejoicing beyond time.

Foes they were, down below
On the common soils that grounded them low
Now they are the angel's troopers of a new dawn
Smoking and drinking in paradise lawn.

In heaven they meet face to face, moment's pause
My Blue and Crimson and their gaze, words at loss
Firm shake of hands, loud was their cheer and laughter
They thanked the Gods, for the smoke on the water.....

X---X---X

Sky Tales

Invading the carpet blue
Decorating in the lonely black
Tattooed east till the blood red west
Waterless ocean on heads that wrests.

That endless beauty has certainly caught
The wandering mind and staring eyes
To plunder the treasures that hold captive
An eternal battle of fire and ice.

Eyes of the beholder have seen these figures
Simple minds with mischievous wagging tails
Romantic hearts on a staged play with dances
The poetic soul scripting those mystical tales.

Deep with meaning and character
A slow flow, ebbing yet captivating
I offered my time for such enigmas to unfold
Oh, that pirate's treasure, beyond the gold.

Beyond the figures and the shapes
Bleeding colors and the falling drapes
Calming the eye and storming the mind
I saw those tales when others were blind...

Tale I

Atop the longest bridge, eyes so still
At the most surreal sight
Written right on the face of dusk
Sketched for the endless bleeding.

Two men after a pot of gold
Fighting and struggling in greed
All in temptation, all for lust
Killing each other, down to dust.

One man's power pushing the other
Both in a struggle in the grainy sand
Breathless a sight, so it was
That mortal wanting, a lost cause.

All of this in the sky, like a stage
Filled with drama in a few minutes
All so moving, only me so still
The rest of the world moves on for its kill.

Tale II

The invasion of a dragon struck true to my next fantasy
With music in my ears, witnessing a war from my balcony

With an army of samurais to the west hiding
A charging creature from the east attacking
It raged its fire on their defenses beyond time
Terrorizing the brave, still playing the waiting
Roaring victorious, it ruled the sky and the lands
Until the soulful assault sent its pride to sands.

The timing was apt for them to arise
From their hiding to get hold and slay
Geared was the army ready was our hero
with the silver sword to slit the prey.

They fought the fire, fought the smoke
Chased the startled dragon, till the floor
With all the courage and their might
They decimated the dragon, by my sight.

Turning to soulful vapors and fading into oblivion
A victory in the sky it was, but battle it was, raging slow
Plan of vengeance, hopes on a numeric high
To avenge its sins, an immortal and eternal cry.

Tale III

A friend once said I witnessed a Biblical tale unfold
One of its own pages from ages old in the skies
As a tale scripted strange, but already written
A rare but new sight, on a high and bitten.

A lady in the sky, afloat in white
Curves and curls, much so apt
A winged soul, faceless and intact.

A rapid change twisted the scene
As she began to fade away to another form
For towards the west, another figure arose
A creature screaming and charging at her.

On sighting danger, she began a transformation
Emerged wings and feathers ready to fly
For the monster had many a head to fight
Dragon it was, with target in its sight.

Turning into a dove, she flew into infinity
Disappearing...cheating the hunter off its prey

A quick chase it was, a hunting tale of centuries old
True to the pages she said, embellished with myths galore.

X---X---X

Dreamcatcher

Nothing to hold on to, except an image…Oh, that mighty bolt from the blue
Opening my shut mind, turning its page…penning the clues to my last
resort.

I fought to catch a fleeting glimpse, for I was not in complete control
I tried to live in that illusionary moment…but fell onto the laps of
reality's roll.

Search I did for a wandering hope, to take me to my dreams that came
A belief that I lived on for now…a sense of relief from this game.

Head hit hard by raw truths and emotions put me to sleep into mere oblivion
There appeared a face and with it, a voice…ghostly, hollow and whispering.

Into the winds they carried my wish, wandering souls, to finally offer
A treat for this wasted mind, fishy…a chance to escape, passenger or
chauffeur.

Eyes closed into momentary hunting
for a want to kill was justified
the living daylights of reality slain
giving it back, its own golden pain.

Caught it was, right by its tail
Hold I did, right by my fist
For a chase it was, hard and fast
A chance to bury the ugly past.

Too quick it was, that lucky catch,
For it raced against time into darkness
Away from my lights of hope and faith
Taking me away to its lair of madness.

I was in flight, high above the land
Fighting my fears in an illusionary battle
Trying to regain my territory's sand
Oh, that serpent with that rattle!

The plan was laid, for the charge
Weapons loaded with courage to barge
A rampaging attack on the enemy lines
At the speed of light, making them blind.

But this was a race against time
Something kept running the wind of caution in my running game
For time had come, the final rain.

It hurled broken images down on me
Rude realities of my crashed past hoping it would deter my ruthless chase
To awake me to a loser's face.

But then I spotted the fatal well
Deep enough to kill this lie, to bury it down beyond the reach of hell
And to seal it forever to let me fly.

I dove pulling its flight, into black and blue
Landed into the haunting black woods in all the green and brown
Yells and hoots filling the spaces, paying its due

A final hold by the neck
Pushing anger and a lasting scream at last...rapid fall for both so fast
One was a crash and another's release from the past.

Hard fall, nearing end
Rival killed, buried fear
Felt free, felt relieved
Uncaged emotions, love released
Sealed well, for good
Reality monster, laid arrest
Battered mind, bruised mine
Solace found, peace bound.
Pursued truth, looking forever
Reality revealed, lies purged
Scary journey, brute route.
Walk now, peace path
Road filled, wishful thinking
Suspense card, handing thrills
Play ready, afraid not.

I wake now from that ride
Into the real world, so true
Where dreams are meant to feel
Where realty is meant to heal.

Haunt not dreams, hunt they will
Snatch not wishes, catch them early
Cry not fate, except bitter truth
Pull not fears, push them away
Walk on ideas, run not out
Fly in dreams, stop not forever
Play in field, cry not alas
Live in life, die not aghast.

Arms wide open to hug
Eyes open wide to sight
Ears open listen to whispers
Mind calls the dream to fight.

You may be on the chariots of time
Chasing the dreams of your life
Riding the wheels turning your fortune
Living on the edge of the knife
Fight a war, a never-ending day
Hold the sun in your hands and play
Catch the stars, come what may.

I awoke not from my dreams
But from nightmares that haunted
Through sleepless nights, with readily served fears
Dumped to the graves, creeping back tears

Closed eyes, opened mind, path to the heart is fine to be blind
Through horizon cutting waters lining the sky,
Take a look beyond that line, take that fall, just try...

X---X---X

Angels On Fire

(An ode to children killed in a fire accident in their school in Kumbakonam, Tamil Nadu, Aug, 2004)

Just beginning their walk on this soil
From the early crawls and the falls
This did not please the power above
Denying them all the joy and love.
Ashened they were with no mercy
Burning tears in wrath filled duty
No way out and no rescue
Sent they were packed in ice.
Creators mourned and cursed the Creators
For this was a sin even for the gods to script
For they hadn't lived a life long
To see their end in a grave like bin.
Spark of the nemesis and its call
Had them in and standing tall
Flames of a circuit consuming their breath
Hopes all choked, calling of death.
Burnt was the soul, not just flesh and bones
Carelessness of inspection cost it all
Denied their visions and desires
Saved from a veiled future's claw.
Now they are laughing and playing
Back in heaven's own guarded gardens
Where all rules are meant to be broken
Where definition and perspective are one.
Oh! God, call them if you want, just whisper
Recall them in peace if you want, do not daunt
Not in pain, but erase their names in silence
For when the fire is out, this smoke forever haunts...

X---X---X

Fading Black

When she arrives just in time
Awake me, to catch my rhyme
Hope to seal a broken gate
Hopes arise, not in smoke, but in hate.

I cry aloud to release the weight
Crack the mirror that in silence, stares
Glare at waters that stand so still
Wish to stamp quick on my kill.

I hear the winds echo a name
Speak of a way, to play the game
A wait it is, in the chill
Poles apart, void to fill.

Oh god, these far lit skies
Dark in shadows I stay
Tales and myths, winds that stray
On the sands of time that play.

Evanescent colors, off the floor,
Something's black, behind the door...

X---X---X

Fallen Angel

Moments fall to memories when they fail
People turn to ashes when they derail
Dreams crash down when they fall
Actions turn to chances, when it is a call.
What happened when he was sent
crashing down, hell bound?
Angering an avenging birth, a punishing mistake
Disobedience causing banishment
Into a world so ugly and tarnished.

He's set a day to stage a comeback, long awaited
A plan schemed under a watchful eye
Preparing for a battle that will wage for long
Gathering an army, slow but sure
Bodies and souls to shatter, to lose count...
A date with his destiny, a mysterious script
Readying a path so bloody no one cares
Where ways and means will have no bounds
Unleashed will be wisdom and so will the hounds

A battle for the throne, a war for the ages
A path to glory, the road to the gates
A field of dreams for one, nightmares to many
An endless journey to an ending fate.

An unseen god to lead from the North
To stop an emerging threat from the South
With pocket full of spells and creatures
Lockets for luck lighting or darkening the future

An epic past reasons the chance of war
A hanging present holds the ground of war
A Fragile future forces the thoughts of war
For it is time what finally runs the war.

All in between may or may not witness history
Some noble soul may pen this day as a story
Paint a picture of chaos with image of collision
Clear the field, reload their rapiers, tend the bloodied

Heaven in white to show the truth, Hell in black to show the brute
One with the light, force to beckon…one from the eternal dark, chance
to reckon.

Sheer authority to question the Gods, utter audacity to seek an answer
by the fallen
A duel due for the deliverance of justice…locking horns for each side's
just reason!

Why did you not bow, when you were told to?
By your beyond, not by your equal…blood cold!
Your refusal to respect the existence of the final truth
Your denial, warranting the reason for your cold fall.

You are 'The Fallen', yet an angel, a title
Not an adversary of any of your past glory
Your hate cannot be justified by reason
For you have been tried for treason.

I've seen you floating in a black cloak
Travelling to corners, gathering your lost pieces
Assembling an army for a mission, I know
A game you decided to play, dice to throw.

You tempt the troops of yours for a motive
Show them an illusion of your desired future
Whereas, a masked reality is what they see
They sell their souls to the one and only thee.

Your form is an infinite image of hollowness
Enchanting even the poets, granting them madness
Spearing into innocent hearts with fear, you lend
Do you intend to fight this battle till the end?
Do you seek an end that will decide your fate?
Mend with pages that have lines already written inside?

Are you still roaming with an unchained army
buying souls that fall to easily and quickly?
Can you sustain to fight this lone battle
with empty tinkers and toys like rattle?
Do you still trust your marching army
to rally along your lonely power?

Oh, fallen angel, are you still in search?
Snatch my face that you could see with
Tear my heart that you could rule with
Seize my mind that you could think with
Haunt my body that you could fight with
Invade my senses that you could feel with
Rage my soul that you could live with
Steal my dreams to wake you off false wits...

Think and attack...for I cannot witness you perish, fall from your stand
For you too are, an angel with a wish to come back home, redeem your land

Oh, 'Son of the Morning', ashore and awake... you might be done at judgment day
Wait not for the final moments to arise...come undone, let us all scream and play

X---X---X

Overture of Departure

Silent skies disturbed by fluttering wings
A purposeful flight invades the void
Signaling a beginning or the end
That went by or is yet to arrive.
Tales come and endings go
Souls that stay, someday have to go
Silent is the journey for some
Some face the eye of the storm.
Tearless cries shed when born
Tear filled eyes when we pass
Last few moments are memory filled
Dripping through holes in our fading heart.
A settling peace after the final road
For the known or unknown is not in our hands
As reason has its own root to ride deep enough
Where fools and even the wise fail to pay heed.
Smoke filled days, light filled nights
More hovers to what meets the eye
For there is something else waiting
That tells you to leave everything behind...
Names stay and so do their stories
To stand the tests of time and tide
All but a smile or a tear falls in the end
A last goodbye, off goes a soul to send...

X---X---X

Reach The Sky, Remember The Earth

Some toil for hunger, some labor for peace
What matters most to me, is that my struggle cease

Some slog for savings, some for the sake of it
Some take the opportunities that knock, only few out of the many

Most see the future to watch the present go by
The best teacher is the past, rarely does one cling to a lullaby

Hearts may break or make, minds may go berserk or bizarre
Play life as a game, break the rules to earn the entitled fame

What matters is the climb to the summit so high
As ladders that reach the sky, are ones only legends tend to fly

We do need to live our lives, for we are already in the flow
Hope not for the worst, as this is the only world in the black glow

Forget not the earth below, remember the sky above
Where beliefs are tested, destiny is handmade and hate mended by love...

X---X---X

The Homecoming

In the Emerald Island's long history
There lies a usual but unknown story
Of young blood snatched away for war
Into bloodied lands for freedom's call.

Pulled away from all horizons... from all his infinite dreams
Called to fight a visible nightmare, a future so black with scars to bear.

Innocent eyes turned bloodshot
Playful hands, taught to kill
Running feet, trained on thorns
Alert ears responded to sirens & alarms.

In that war, one side was the migrant settlements seeking their rights
and grants
A battered nation, on the coin's other side, a hunt for peace against the
tiger's brunt.

A fight for what they called freedom
On an island, a heaven on earth
Under leaders with their goal
With that, a hole in their soul...

Years of training had finally passed
Put through the anvil and the hammer
Preparing a premature funeral, the final blow
A move that would finally stage his show.

He prepared for facing his demons
In the heat, cold and in the unforgiving rains
His body and mind bending in all degrees
Molding his art of war, beyond chains.

He shunned away the fear of death
For he sought an eternal honor
If life lived, it was seen as selfish
Pride was in penance and sacrifice to perish.

Their philosophy, forced his mind
To think of heavens, after death
For now he lived a hell on the earth
Where for glory, he was given birth.

He prepared for the longest days
Eagerly waited in the darkest corners for hours
Patiently counted his running out few minutes
Yearning for a battle that would last for seconds.

But our man was pushed to the death squad
Assigned to the suicide bombers for a faster glory
Shocked he was at the decision so fast
For dreams of the new infinite, broken at last.

Skepticism hovered over his troubled head
For a quick death, was not his cup
Plans crashed, avalanched rapidly
Questions invaded his struck mind.

In all the smoke and the steel of the battlefield
He agreed to march along with fading hopes
From a chance to create history with a waging war
To a swift fall to another grave, nameless and faceless.

Mortal fears, now came alive…and so did his weakness show
For eternal doors were too far from reach…as another conflict shadowed.
Battle between the mind and heart, a choice too hard to make his day
Shopping for options and chances, he sought his rendezvous to live another way.

The tiger's departure to battle was a silent tradition, a secret meeting at the shores
Where probable martyrs met their kith, kin and soul-mates to convey their wishes

Hugs and kisses, some agreed while some disagreed under the bathing moonlit waters
A chance they have in this practice where a thin red line separates their fates

A final choice, where they prowl back to the Warfield to their waiting destroyers.
Or return to their haven's bosom to seek peace and yet honor their legionnaire loyal

The one who crosses that thin red line is a free man and is gifted with his rights
For he is free to choose his walk of life but has to forego the ways of the bloodying knife.

Our man was on the wait for this moment...a chance to reconcile a crazy decision
A wise way out from broken dreams, snatched innocence's price paid in submission

That fateful night had finally arrived, where a line would judge an end
An end to death or a life, a beginning, beyond the art of the warring knife.

The call letter knocked his doors, ending his patient penance
For a long silence was finally broken with their welcoming gates, thrown open.

They knew, they had one last chance to call him back to home with renewed hopes
They proceeded to the shores on time, waited along the sands standing in line

The whispering waves hushing his name from the temporary tides
The howling winds in racing memories where 'innocence' was his name.

He then came walking, from a distance...an incoming vision lighting their eyes
His smiling colors filling the void, fulfilling their only wish with a much needed buoy.

Absent words gave way for emotions, the eyes said it all
Expressions and gestures, defined their feelings 'et all

For a comeback was most awaited
Not of a hero, but a son so debated.

Their fears and tears called him back home
Their arms pleaded and outstretched...

But that line separated their fate
A thin line between love and hate.

The sea beyond, gave its call
For it was the final rendezvous

A call before dusk's pall
A choice to define his rise or fall

Time he took, saw his brothers and sisters behind
A step he took, two, to seal his fate and calm his mind

Reaching beyond destiny's line, to wipe the tears of his hate.
Embracing love, wiping out the signs of worry and haste

A place called home in a war, so invisible
Was a home that invited peace so invincible.

His comrades saw him choose his way...a freedom of choice, their tradition
A culture before the war's near dawn where a petal, fights to see the sun in the lawn.

They too shared the smiles for he chose to follow his heart into heavenly haven
The art of war was no more his...death was now the birth of a life renewed

Scenes of bloodied soils and metal riddled souls was now beyond sight
A memory that will still remain as an act of the past at its height

Even the distant guilt ran away, healing wounds with a fading pain.
For a home got back its son...for a son got back his home.

The lonely starry night sought its moon, an age old romance
The yearning sands soaked its violent and passionate tide
The empty dens rejoicing the hunter's valiant and unsure return,
This was a tale of his fateful one-way ticket's thrilling return ride...

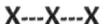

X---X---X

The Last Stand

Oh, men of honor I salute you in your sun
For my words burn in your glory of the past
Time might have buried your rein by the gun
But immortal signs keep it alive, still on the run.
I have turned the pages of history and time
And traveled through the tales and fables
In search of mysteries of this world so real
When I discovered the might of your steel.

The fall of legends, the end of their day
The reason & truth too less in dismay
God knows, where the last lights fell
Your secret treasure for the world to tell.
Protector of the emperor's land & people
Power and pride of the nation's repertoire
Keeper of word, seeker of the flame
Born for honor, death for the mortal endgame.
You stand as a pillar of a long lost clan
Maybe planning in heaven of a mighty comeback
For your blood still flows in your rivers and lands
For your soul still braves and guards innocent hands.

In the last stand of your final resistance
Till the last drop had soaked in the field
A sacrifice the enemy saw in the far end
Shattering the legendary and mighty shields.

The swing of the steel to the fearing skin
The scream of calling death a bloody sin
The charge of the sword, in for the kill
The emperor's final move, up the hill.

They say it was an end so brave...honor held intact and unbroken
With the winds that carried your souls to the gates of heaven
Even the gods had kept it open to welcome you with arms open

Outnumbered, yet ready to die...for a reason, a touch too high
Charging with a handful of men
Into the jaws of death without a sigh.

The final leap at the enemy's neck, the charge at the enemy's lines
The final sight of friends and foes
The final slash, the ending signs.

Unhappy with the decision to dismantle caused dismay
An age old system that existed in a mist of myths
The shroud over the emperor's vision proclaiming for a change
A decision that would conclude an era, as simple as sin...end an age

The siege of the garrison was the only win...a brave attempt, a rebellion
as per plan
But a heavy loss was what hit hard...that's where they played the wrong
card

The six-week battle pushed them to *Shiroyama* after a blunder to give
the only time
For the imperialist army to finalize the blow, a fatal move to end their
raging show.

The pushback up the mighty hill from *Kumamoto* was enough on the
bill to settle
Stopping not a final battle at hand to see...they had a hope of a victory,
in eternity.

Waiting they were for a call from above that would reunite them with
their gods
Who wrote in their fates with honor that rode on their backs, a promise
to their abode.

In the fields of peace so green enchanting
A deathlike stillness hovered… taunting
Towards the west was the equipped army
On the east, a handful of warriors, waiting.

The winds whispered the call of the moments
Their prayers knocking the doors of hope
Gripping their weapons, the only chance
Their life's last battle, their last dance.

Weapons of the west, kept in hiding
Waiting to strike in the right timing…
For a motive too was kept in the covers
For its revelation was a key in firing.

The Westward troopers marched to the beat
The Eastward warriors positioned on horsebacks
With bows and arrows, swords and spears
They prepared to fight speeding steel and invisible fears.

The call was given, the charge was ordered…running feet and galloping hooves
Blinding colors and smoke of war eclipsing the sun,
The symphony of destruction had finally begun.

The bloodiest final battle ever was fought
All in a day's end, the swiftest of all
The saddest end to an everlasting thought
The final horn, to cease the charging calls.

The end was silent with a quiet kill
Seppuku of honor, final tradition, uphill
No prisoners, for there was no man standing
No suffering, for it was the last stand falling

Saigo, the last hero, the General to many
Pardoned he was posthumously and re-ranked
Given the honor post the showdown
A move by Emperor *Meiji* on home ground.

A final salute and the honor bow
Was a signal to the bloodiest end
Of how a clan must take vow
A final stand, message to send.

O! Those slashing swords that outshine the rising sun
In the skies where they now belong, before the age of guns

An abode for their souls now far and beyond reach, scripted only in pages
A defense wall that was once beyond breach, now famed in tales for
the ages...

X---X---X

The Element

Born from the fire of an eternal flame
Burning bed, an entire game
Fighting ablaze, facing the same
Oh! That smile in the devil's name

Floating in the shores of long lost time
We swim across the oceans of deep
Drowning the sins of yours and mine
We dwell in mortal sublime, neck deep

Carrier of minds, machines and mynahs
Releases my soul from this caged hall
For I yearn to count the stars till I die
Betray me not like Icarus while I fly

Born in the sands of a homely cry
I crawl and lie, walk and run
Sowing hope with a wanting eye
Below the feet is where I return...

I look above to watch the fall of hate
From your throne to witness mortal man dictate
Open mystery from colors to shapes
The math is irrelevant, the sun is on its way

We are one...the element of truth
True is the element in me and you...

X---X---X

Nail on the coffin

Broken glass from a shattered hope
Dark smoke from a burning dream
Quick sands sucking to the depths
Whirlpool waters churning alive
Whirlwind swooping from all ends
Deluge sweeping all from above
Torrent wave pulling to the abyss
Dissipating air choking the scene
Colors vary from spectrum wide
Sounds fade and deafen to defy.

Shots are in, strikes are out
Rock walls close in, squeeze and spout
Striking bolts, from the black and blue
Storms in command, picking on you
Piercing rain, cutting in through
Once were tales, myths were lies
Wish the end had more merciful eyes.

Walk was a run, rust was the car
Hot was the day, cold was the night
Deep was the wound, divine was the pain
Set was the stage, tragic was the scene

Then, a wake-up call...alarmingly close
Splash on the face, to smell the rose
Pinched to pain, it all seemed far away
The calm was comforting, to face the day.

Tears were gone, so was the pain
Sweat filled palms pursing to pray
Wishing not to dream again in slumber
For my cradle was graved six feet under...

X---X---X

Foot-Notes

A voice yells out, ready to address the pairs
The leader of the stinky rack waits and pacifies all
You'll miss this conference if you shut the doors
Hold on a bit, wait till you hit the floors.

"Shoved we are, stamped we are
Tracked and tread in terrible terrain
Rain, heat, sweat or cold
We are not taking this anymore!
This is a massacre! An insult parade...
Do we participate in this masquerade?

Human activities are a stamp of authority
Wearing us wherever they please, in or out
Stoned and thorny, paths, pits and potholes
Slippery and skating, fast, trod or crawl.

Assisting in violence for assault and insult
Smashing of lesser beings to pulp
Kung-fu kicks for fancy or defense
Intimidate irrespective of gender bias!

Call us romantic for we never part the pair
Wherever we are lost, temple, church or mosque
Call us societal footmarks, for we standard your living
Aren't we those who give back and forth, summer or spring?

We may be branded or pirated! Cheapest and pricey at times...
Tough for a soldier and weakest to the strata that doesn't care
Privileged to have stepped on holy lands & crossed many a bridge
Do we deserve the hospitality you serve us with disdain and dismay?

All we ask is respect as to a certain degree for we are near to perfect
We can sweep off your adept feet with deft touch and elegance
Leave you reeking with utter shame or bleed you to black
So when we save your skin, better scratch ours, or we'll bite back..."

The General's speech concluded as he hung off in slow motion
'A dead rubber' screamed one from the corner, triggering a commotion
For what began as an appeal to the taller being, ended with a mutiny
As they stamped and stomped in lined up racks, awaiting a heathen destiny!

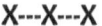

X---X---X

Day One Dark...

Walking and patting the cane
He did stroll for a reason
Not only to know which lane
But to feel, which season.

All he could see was night
A friend for solace from outer space
So many questions in mind
A constant hunt for answers, his chase

All he sought was to feel
The light of hope in the darkness
Sound of the drops, ripple shape madness
Not the color of the waters or of the skies
Before feeling a manhole in swiftness.

Remembering the sounds of his past
A recovery within, rare moment to console
But as usual, the future did cast a doubt
A question mark strolling with him.

Wanting to find home, he was
Lost he was, unusual directions
Roaming where the ears led him
Before a voice halted his mad run.

A voice, mother like affection
Led him to his usual path, usual scent
Familiar he thought...that voice and smell
A bolt from the blue, roll of the dice.

Lost her early, fond memories
Leaving him to fend for himself
Act of survival, his only ticket
A well taught mind, his safety kit

Back to his haven, key under the carpet,
Groceries galore, feast for his dinner
May have friends or neighbors drop in
Or just fill his glass for a solo act of sin.

With laughter aloud and cries of sadness
That familiar voice, lost smell and hidden essence
Gave him a final reason to hope and feel
For a godless future with no reason to kneel...

X---X---X

Soldier of the Sun

Clawing in hunger
On star mapped roads
I seek the hands of thee
To beg and borrow in sorrow...

I write to my tune
Rhyme & reason don't seem to fuse
The sun is screaming for my soul
Reason to roam, roam and roam...

Can't catch me, I am the wind
Wanderer...dreamer

I count the lines on the dunes
Ripping my path in rage
Fed me lies for ages
Laced in books I once raided

Born like this, roaming black and light
Before you see, I am gone
On some day, I will end this fray
I will deal with my god, one way

Come roam with me, on the run,
I am the soldier of the sun!

X---X---X

Mirror, Mirror On The Wall

Show him the darker side
The one who stares
Reveal to me, who's on the ride
On whose face those look wears.
He shows a lighter side
And hides the plain truth
Has he got an idea or a plan
To set the devil free?
What is in that mystic mind?
Only you know through the wall
Make him realize, he's blind!
That soon he shall finally fall.
Make him stare into his own eyes
And face his darkness,
Exorcise his demons.
Let him try to break the ice
And unearth the ugliness.
A gentleman among thousands
And a smile to top it all
He creeps down on all ends
To peek and listen to secret calls.
Like a ruling king in full force
A gladiator fighting for freedom.
He is the shadow, the truth
The lightning among the rain clouds
The knife in a gunfight shootout
The answer to the haunting doubts.
Tell him, I shall wait...for a confrontation, tall
Tell him, don't be late...Oh mirror, mirror on the wall!

X---X---X

Dirty Money

Tempting times, desperate need
Selling soul, false missions
Opening eyes, shutting mouth
Turning heads, running legs
Stretching hands, punching air
Talking talk, walking walk
Hire and fire, smiling terror
Selling seats, sorry cases
Smoking guns, hand grenades
Running politics, hiding files
Turning blames, faulty towers
Clean grounds, sewer below
Antique wine, suffering child
Sports car, rolling wheels
Dark skies, smoky pipes
Rolling dice, hiding cards
Hit men, guns plenty
Big targets, petty crimes
Lengthy ramps, cool sets
Super models, billboard spots
Heavy purse, gentleman
Cell phones, nice ride
Palatial villas, hiding place
Visiting cards, credit cards
Heavenly bond, shaggy end

Endless soaps, game shows
False pride, long life
Material world, open obsession
Nexus crises, endless wars
Rising leaders, falling heads
Cloning hell, oil pipes
Falling missiles, wrong targets
Death cry, missing notes
Burnt heaven, lost soul
Roaming peace, hidden solutions
God given, man made
Fading mother, desperate cries
Striving father, enigmatic son...

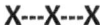

X---X---X

Welcome Waters

Colorless bulbs hang on my gates
Rippling the world around me
Awakening the reflections of a stagnant life

The gentle breeze carrying me far away
Into the skies of a new tomorrow
Dealing with the demons of yesterday, unfolding life today

The drop on the cracked skin, distracting
The drops on the forehead, motivating
The writings on the soil, awakening
The mirage on the road, reflecting

The song of the trees when they sway
Gifted rhythm and ghostly howl
The dance of the green fields, draped and mopped

The smile of a child on the run
The sight of joy, when masking the sun
The arrival of friends, and the subsequent cup of tea

The joy of players, when it leaves the fields
The battle and struggle, a clean fight turned ugly
Cleansed it is now with a scent of hope, play resuming.

Close my eyes now and wait on my terrace
Savoring the sights of a rumbling and cracking sky above me
On the cusp of an immortal dream, an eternal echo hugs in frenzy

Mother to the child, Father to the farmer
Brother to the soldier, Sister to the weak
Cupid to the lover, muse to the artist
Hope to the dying, Emperor to the people
Enemy of the mercury, killer the living
Friend of the petals, ending the penance.

Welcome they are in time of need, but not in rage
Antagonize her not, for it is pure and flown by an unseen power
Up above the world so high, like a firing tank in the sky!

X---X---X

Mother, Dear...

From the gates of birth
To the jaws of death
Giver of soul, taker of breath
I held a hand, but she held my heart.

From open doors to every corner
I roam into unending time
On the horizon, she is the shadow of mine.

Accepting our pains and stains
Adoring every moment and scene
She still stands there waiting for you
In home lands, where hope is your food

Sacrificing her hunger for your cry
Throwing away her thirst, to dry
A shelter under the sun and rain, healer of pains

Schooling the way of life in subtle ways
Hard lessons nailed in the head as well
Waiting for your walk and talk, a marvel in all
She exists in some form, when you take that fall

May be close or oceans afar
Her thoughts are always on you
Make sure you distance not and forget not

The holy kitchen, her imaginary tales
Her cajole in pain, the chiding gaze
The cries heard in silence or aloud
The only voice till death parts and beyond.

Rush home to that waiting heart, despair not
Feel the warmth of the bosom, seek not anywhere else
Whatever religion, she is the only living god to have set afoot, grace!

X---X---X

Vasanth Kumar J

True That!

An enigmatic path that finally leads, but
Through knee deep minefields and trenches

A path crossed by few, backed with courage
Witnessed by the gods, while others simply crack.

Only the true warrior treads on this path
Does not deter on the rugged route of this dart.

There are no friends to stand beside
For it is to blend with the dark when the light goes dim.

In today's bitter world where the truth is still elusive
Selfish are battles and means are repulsive.

A day shall finally arrive, the world will certainly face
The consequence of a thousand lies, the laws would fear to chase...

X---X---X

Final Field

He waits with his hands in prayer
For a drop to fill his lands
Fooled he was, for not once
In a wait that tore his strands.
He wandered from east to west
Roaming eyes, searching for hope
Beating heart, nearing the rope
Hungry souls, healed by dope
Wanting minds, on the slope.
'They' in silence, on the distant corners
Serving the world that silences him
Ignoring his cries that shattered slim
By the noise of the bruised and battered.

Every morning another night
Every wait another end
Every hope, ending in dismay
Every chance, another play.
He, for once chose to script his fate
And sat on his field's resting place
With a final throw of the dice
A chance he took, an end he saw twice.
Fasting till the end, a final fight
An eternal challenge, a price ready to pay
Held the motherly sands in his palm
A ticking clock he would lest forget to wake.

The only music was of the ghostly winds
Ordering him to back off, for chances were slim
Refuse he did, chanting a name he believed
For ages that answered, but were now bereaved.
He felt in days, his breath slow down, drying up
Eyes soaking into his own seas of disbelief
Shivering hands, clenching to the shimmering sands
First held, from the day he dreamt of hope.
With an end drawing nearer, he held tight his life
A walk on the knife, hand held prayer and sigh
About to shed his last tear, a final cry for the family's due
A warrior clad descended in shades and hues, ghostly *Yama*.

He stood with all his final might, creaking bones
Preparing for the final stand he had, sagging veins
For he welcomed a death that greeted
Ended a birth that floored from heaven.

'They' descended in all their might to carry his soul away
To the gates he only dreamt of, wish of a simple man
At last he played with god and won his pending strife
A noble struggle for the earth's children, a worthy life

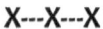

X---X---X

Live To Die Another Day...

Seven days, twelve months
One religion, many monks
Fate defined, destiny deciding
Feeding foes, devil's residing
Social fight, anger pored
Past regrets, remorse flowed
Lost chances, still air
Comeback's awaited, worthy dare
Dark knight, next is bright
Deep wounds, fighting stand
Rival's laughter, wanting cries
Blood spent, never denied
First crawl, run forever
First pangs, feast famine
Struggle within, blinking eye
Lonely peak, firing line
Smile forever, innocence lost
Long walk, cutting cost
Sighting beauty, racing heart
Green forever, cooling sun
Long wait, branded watch
Time's yours, on song
Win hearts, far afield
Cut tail, snap horns
Push sword, face fear
Pierce hard, go near
Win war, not battle
Live death, die alive...

X---X---X

Vasanth Kumar J

Storm Child

I saw you as a child in my arms
When you came into my life
A past you had, I had shelter to
Protected your neck from the knife.

Time passed by and you inched a few
With the world around turning anew
Sensed a distance that was to come
Failed to see your freedom run

I stand now wanting your hand,
For you have gone away
A freedom that tares me apart,
The choking end of our song

I stare into those eyes in photographs
Like you did, back some time
For the same hands now hold me responsible
And cage me for an unjust crime, the crucible

I now stand waiting for the sun to rise, for another day
I sing to the winds that lift me, to forget and move away

I will look out for the storms, like in you
Commit not the same mistake twice
Walk I shall into the eye
Embrace what comes to me alive

Child I am now, for you too were once
Too early you grew up, too far now
For a spark stroked this burning fire
Engulfing to end this burning desire.

I wait for the strike of time, patiently
Deafening gongs ringing in the memories
For only few stand the test of Father Time,
In anguish, standing tall...yearning your rhyme.

X---X---X

Blind Cut

Tripped through…stripped you
Tough clue…with you
Dark night…black sky
Your arms…hold me tight
Push my mind…to the wanting eyes
Oh…it's your love…that sets me right…
Take me….to the silent night
Hold me…in deepened sight
Touch me…to pause my fight
Far away from this blight.
Caught you…held heart
Hanging from the waging start
Words cut…torn down
Pages turn…broken ground
Time flies…fire flies
Roaming soul…loving lies
Loud calls…last rites
Last breath…falling skies
Push my mind…to wanting eyes
Your words…make me high
Take me…to the howling pack
Hold me…till they pry me open
Touch me…to wake the shepherd
Feed me…myths unspoken and unheard.

X---X---X

Spirit Today

Stereotypes hitting the floor
Smoking guns killing the air
Doped souls filling the void
Tearing wheelers rip the road
Pierced skinners ink the kin
Branded hippies tread the streets
Painted wheels pimp for mates
Technology filling the empty pocket
Desired hands eloping the world
Power hungry minds score the nulls
Wordy kids mouth their way on-stage
Purpose filled legs pursue till the kill
Hungry hearts eat till they drop dead
Perverted desires haunt the innocent
Hollow souls for one night's pleasure
Broken hearts taking it to needles
Tender failures see not the sunset
Drowned memories at lonely gates
Wanting hands hoping for a friend
Betrayed heart now seeks a friendly foe
Young pockets blinded by paper plastic
Growing desires by violent possessions
Sloshed nerves dampened by spirit
Trampled chances, meet of the fists

Fashions aged minus the basics
Shy past to a bold today, bare tomorrow
Homeless and hopeless to desperate means
Worshipping madness as a new God
Retorting history and roaring religions
Digital walls with names painted on them
Fear of privacy, glass shattering scream
Peaceful today, scaring tomorrow
Evolutionary paths, emerging philosophies
Where are we heading to, where are we now?
Could you please turn on the lights…are we in or out?

X---X---X

Rush Hour

Crossed minute and hour arms, swords set for battle
Defying the alarm that screams, snoozed to charge
Shutting off the sun piercing our eyes, flags mast
The slumber is the enemy in any waning dream.

Rushing to the waters, a race of wits
Chaos of common grounds scripted
Men on duty, lyric of a daily song
For when time nears, lines snake along.

Then the moment of hunger to break the fast
Killing of the wanted eyes, a temporary death
Rush to the hall, witness a merciless round table
The greedy banishing horses of the same stable

Untied knots and flying collars, tucking shirts and fasten boots
Running fast, from the morning jog to the concrete and glass
Morning routine riposte with bunker mates and neighbors too
First minutes of the mantra between concentration and distraction

Transit dreams to fade away into
Snoring under the pages that convey
Ringing bells, wrap of set, rush of minds
Tick tock, another crash course blinds

Another run, in the sun
Notes and tests, under the gun
Pouring sweat, struggle to glory
Tough days, blinded ugly
Musical chairs, way of life
World it is, on the knife
Tasteless lunch, burning dessert
Swallow not bite, silencing munch
Word with friends, rumor updates
Ignorant to the bell, hate this fate.

Assignments load, invasion of the labs
Musical chairs, child's play that stabs
An adult's world, seeking answer for grades
Submission time, mercy of the master's raids

Evening hangouts till the sinking night
Pre-midnight post-mortem, the day that died
Minutes to hours, hours to another day
Realizing the sun is yet to kick start another play
Second serving, repeat rush, gear for push and pull
Friend and foe on the move, life it is...half glassful.

X---X---X

Nothing's Lost

It's a funny game we all play
From every field to every ground
Side to side, east to west
Top to bottom, north to south

There have been calls off the edges
Close moments that decide fall or glory
Rise and fall of a hero facing his fate
By the nemesis who too patrons this hate

The doubting hero who nearly but touches not
Peak of a temporary form, undoubted class permanent

Always a chance to prove a comeback is potent
To kick the past and shove aside the killing drug
There is always another game to play and prove
There is always another whistle that calls true

It's worth that tread back to the track, where it all began
Passionate dreams driven by time and practice
There is no harm to dream for glory again, at any stage
We will fall due to a blinding ego, an unchecked rage

Spirits present to back, for none like riding alone
Kith, kin, friend or foe, chanting that name, slow
For the game is always bigger than the player
A philosophy, a mission, the bigger picture

Real it is, the pursuit is tougher than the goal
Truth it is, the chase is harder than the kill
Fear it is, on the roads of a returning soul
But fight it is, to overcome the demon's will.

On your feet my friend, arise and awake
Nothing is lost, all for a reason for now or forever
Take that field, run that track, hit that lever
The world is waiting for a story to cure the fever...

X---X---X

Open Arms

Spirit on a high, sky at a low
Moments with you so, so slow
Life on the edge with these times
World full of hope, dope and shine...

Come home to open arms
I call your name for I'm at alms

Lights on the streets that spot us
On the roads of our past, that knight us
Secret meetings in the night and silent love
Can we relive and retake those scenes?

Hoping you would come home to open arms, aching in absence
I yearn for the rain in dry lands, akin to your, once a presence

Stars counted every day and random verses penned
Echoing in my mind and heart, the promises in the nights
Dreams where we saw oceans part and The Lochness float

Hoping you would come back to open arms, holding the door open
For I see a gaping moment come alive, broken locks and mood soften...

Life is on the edge, Oh love...hanging by a thread
For I am here, I am now...grant me life or give me death...

Come home to open arms
I call your name for I'm at alms...

X---X---X

Walk on, fight on…

Fight of the sun against the colossal clouds
To rise from the east everyday

Flight of the birds for the winds that clout
Where the skies are the only runaway

Wander of the nomad and his ship against the elements
To the oasis that brings peace and shade

Brittle buds braving a raging storm
The bloom that often wins the battle.

The diseased too fight and cheat death
Cradle or grave is where truth will bed

The wild too fights men, guns and bullets
Guerilla warfare scaring the poacher, hunt stalled

Inner demons withholding our forgiveness for guilt
Crack the ego for humble surrender, poles will tilt

If your way is barraged, forget not to break the fence wide
If the storms flood the day, forget not to sail and glide
The dirt may hide our sight, forget not to wipe it clear
March on my soldier, it is war…do not cry, everyone dies!

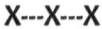

X---X---X

Impromptu

The aroma that connects and pulls wishes together
The color that crashes the gates of all nations
Warm friend and a companion to the falling drops
Sip of one for more to come, the brewing spirit of life

A barren desert with the circling sun
The nomadic heart that beats a lone rhythm
An empty paper with a story to tell
A temple of gods with no priest to bell...

A knight from the darkest emotions that arose
A winning heart that runs despite defeat or dose
A simple but deep dream that chases me all along
This life is but a journey with a background song...

Lovable soul from deep within, a beauty from beyond
A thousand leagues in her eyes, a flash of lightning
A mother's heart embodied in adolescent eyes
A hand to hold, the eyes to fall, a smile to die for...

A thousand words with the nod of the head
A single meaning with the dip of the eye
An unexplainable mystified emotion of Eve
The epic love shrunk in one biting moment

Failing balance spilling me in every direction
A splitting head like a friction set fire
A rampaging river from the temples above
Rising mercury signaling the need for love

I fare thee well into a world of tomorrow
Forget not us, who have sailed with you,
For our memories will forever remain,
With a fistful of hope that shall float anew…

Remember that this is just the beginning
Of a journey that may take you places
Fear not what may come in your way
Godspeed to you, with a pocket full of aces

X---X---X

Midnight Muse

The brightest carpet in the darkest of times
Laid out on the belly of the rumbling beast
An orchestrated motif that fills the lair
Witnesses constellated in pick and pair.

A tale woven by connecting the dots
In an empty page of an infinite all
Shaded in white by the arrival of the pearl
The muse is mine and she hears my call.

I request her to narrate a tale in awe
But she deep dives into patient eyes
By my hands, into my world so raw
She takes me beyond love and lies.

Uncovering my thoughts, screening them alive
The tale runs in the skies, giving me the blues
Discovering my dreams, keeping them alive
She collects them all, they must be groomed.

She leaves before I could ask her any further
All she does is smile and promises another
In abated breath she fades away into the black
I wait now forever until my muse is back...

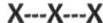

X---X---X

Vasanth Kumar J

The Reunion

Time tests the wits of those
Who play their ways into foes
But friends succeed when together
Stitching a time in bad weather.
Chances take us far, beyond the line
But there is a hand to reach us in time
For we meet again, away from madness
Historic reunions, partners in crime.
Varied colors in us that display
Of what we were and are today
Uncanny antics that remind us all
That being together is a mighty call
From teachers to the taught
Mates who bled and fought
A rare mix we are, a gang of one
Oh! Those days, glorious and undone
Laughter and speech, loud and clear
Drink and food, wiping the tear
Welcoming the year hand in hand
Brothers we are, of the marching band...

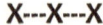

X---X---X

Closing End

Covered skies, simple walk
Weak limbs, feeble talk
Turning back, standing shock
Historic age, crumbling rock
Wanting hands, invisible reason
Telling times, unseen season
Torn conditions, portraying treason
Dismayed scene, foolish poison
Blackened white, whitened black
Time ahead, sorrow's back
Empty pockets, filled sack
Filled eyes, empty shack
Placed tiles, sand piles
Stoned cushion, fireflies
Open dreams, ending times
Own blood, life of lies
Open street, open hope
Fallen angel, living dope
True figure, sad soap
Desperate prayer, burning rope...

X---X---X

V for...

Speak to be heard
Act to undo
Yield not to outdo
Right to all
Left, right or center
Male, Female or Trans
Worship stone or spirit
Eat the living or the dead
Care to win, be a sport
Girl child, right to be safe
Women safety, last agenda

Fluctuating prices, economic warfare
Loan & debt, losing farmers
Chemical laced, false certificates
Dumping the rivers, new packaging
Depleting ozone, hole in the sky
Climate change, shifting monsoon
Awaiting families, parched throats
Urbanization, emptying villages
Tilled land, dug up foundations
Census statistics, baffling vacancies
Leaders blank, speech without data
Bluffing and blames, self before nation
Curfews and ceasefires, ready, aim...fire
Women fighter pilots, women make-up artists
Zero knowledge, spot speeches
Tolerance levels, laurels returned
Random comment, burning homes
Apologies accepted, position debated
Eating habits, wasting disgust
Mid-Day menu, bent for fools

White goods, black money
Blue collar, white authority
Expanding estate, fallen forests
Legacy of the hand, power of the flower
Communal existence, questioning today
Tender relations, words that trigger
Act of brothers, nations unite
Supporting sentiments, alignment denied
Quotas & Castes, opportunities yearned
Forward or backward, common sense defied
Open policies, urban impact
Unseen picture, rural unchanged
Child marriage, superstitions
False prophets, guarded priests
Organized poverty, cartelized mafia
Population explosion, race agenda
Investment finance, educational bias
Capital punishment, barbaric acts
Grades and ranks, suicidal pressure
Social recognition, selfie centric experience
Impressing the next, forgetting oneself
Groupthink in, individualism out
Points for quotient, excuses for character
Salary for degrees, penniless for the arts
Human resources, body shopping
Importance to machines, no care to man
Cost per capita, costly mistake
Merged and acquired, sacked and packed
Subjective discussions, objective ignorance
Open information, access denied
Net neutrality, exiled for exposing
Corporate funding, government agenda
Modern practices, close minded bodies
Awards returned, strangled artists
Fundamental rights, constrained fights
Muscled backing, bold statements
Common man, weak when divided
Conservative mind, progressive pretense
Vocal to change, no right to preach

Signs of emerging capitalist, future thinking
Where are the socialist and the secular?
Where are the democratic and the sovereign?
Identity transition, deep rooted change in question
Should we yield to parties with shifting impression?

This is my country, exciting isn't it?
We get to taste the good, bad & ugly.
I say we break those lines that divide
Erase the beliefs that defy common sense
Abandon madness for reason, take that path
Bar all the shortcuts, cage all the corrupt
Listen more, talk less, give a heart and lend a mind
Pro-poor for poverty eradication
Anti-rich for societal iteration
Shake hands with the enemy,
Spare not the traitor for treason
Kill no time for a passing act
Breach not borders, for we will rebel
Seek not the other's oil or diamonds
Push for alternative solutions
Renew, recycle, refresh and reflect
Can't do it on my own, cannot do it with you
Join hands, mend hearts, mold beliefs, sync not lips
Find the right soul, seek the one...
Better the search, worth the journey
Put not on stage, but place amongst us
For no one is higher or lower than the other
Make the choices that ultimately matter
Impact for this nation, else She will suffer
Vote to veto...veto not to vote
The solution is not in running away
The fight is to live another day...

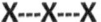

X---X---X

U-Turn

When the winds of change fill the minds
That in deep slumber, has rusted over time
A light beckons in the misty eyes that blink
To the skies that call to turn a new leaf.
I now awake hoping for better times
For the black in me has faded into oblivion
I am now white in the deep sea of emotions
For even the grey has taken its seat.
From the devils bend to the angels garden
The transition from the depths to a newfound reach
Lighting the darkest fears with the colors of hope
Far away from the chancing the jump and beseech
I now arise from the electric chair
And gag my past in those arms and tied
Watch it melt and erase an old score
Giving me a present in my wanting hands.
A sunrise to every sunset, dawn to dusk
A smile to every tear, sorrow to joy
A journey to every halt, now or never
A life to every death, hope forever.
I now face old roads, once hated
I now hold bound head, once hung
I now beat the heart, once cursed
That life is a ride worth the fun.
No more, the fool in the garden
No more, the puppet in others hands
No more, the loner near the corner walls
I am now the soul that welcomes the call
Watch me sail across the seven seas
Diving deep in flooding emotion that sped
Time to set my scores right, for the good
No point in escaping the calling bed...

X---X---X

Calling Fields

I ripple the water so still
Along with the falling drops
To assure myself of a moment
That nears close to keep me fill
I run about dancing with friends
And with foes in their merry fights
A calling mother warning from afar
To keep away from what pleases me
Close memories that I always cherish
I wrap it up in my arms and let it fly
In the skies of freedom that are clad
A paradise that only few can sight
I make my boats that row in the winds
In ponds that are deep but calm
I dig paths for rivers on the barren lands
Give life to deathly cracks with hands.
I sing my songs of the rains
That call the ages together in merry
To enjoy what passes by as a stranger
Coming back in an uncertain ferry
I drink the water of the skies
That nature has quenched this child
A mother who waits for us in worry
At our doorsteps, yearning voice
I live this moment even at a lost age
Where we see the rains through a cage
Worrying about an unsure event
That once we lived in, that thrill.
With our gear and guards marching
We invade the fields that flood the heart
That sight of joy filled lands
Warnings now of another storm
An event of play, laughter and fun
Amongst the dirt and the slush

Where the garden once lay plush
And called for our fleet to rush.
The days of the fearless souls
Now years of the feared and cowered
Once a playground to rule and conquer
Now a field to be swallowed and vanquished.
I hope to step back onto this field with friends
To defy the myths of the past hangs as a portrait
To ripple the silent waters not alone, with due company
Longing hope of another childhood coming alive...

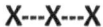

X---X---X

On The Edge...

The world we know now hangs on a thread
Rusting values painted anew, renamed

With silence playing hard
The game is to pick the right card

The age old survivor too tells a tale
Scripted on the face, from fresh to pale.

All towards the same destination
But differing paths at every station

Goals differ, targets grow, companies change
Strangers will turn companions, friends will estrange

Some for paper and some for an inner fire
Worth the shedding sweat and tear, warranting a smile

There are some dreams that still remain
Like painted clouds that hardly rain

Brick made castles, floating are most
All it takes to prove character is a raging storm

The world around us may be a heaven or hell
Will you clay and claw to make it worthy to tell

Reading between the lines is perfected when an art
Sketch or scratch, a poem's edge stitches or tears a life apart...

X---X---X

My Dear Madras...

Singara Chennai, Marina's home
Built in sand, silt and stone
Tougher weather bound, rougher animated folk
Moments filled and memories abound

Sunrise on the shore, kicks of proceedings
Pictures on the table, hanging on the wall
Splash of the water, light of the camphor
Pungent incense and mystic *Kolam* chores
Movie like scenes, many a director's call

Town of the shrines, bell of the gods
Land of the chants and holy verses
Sands of the culture, politically rooted
Fisherman folk origins, the sailing coast
Housing boards and slums that surround
Alcoholic revenues, in and behind bars
Street sports ruling the rage sans the age

Headlines and journals that wake and update
Propaganda and posters donning free walls
Tea & Kaapi stalls, stands feeding at dawn
Screaming vendors proving their product
Meals and Biriyani that define the mid-day
Street food, deep fry, Burmese & pickle dry
Movie songs and FM on public transit modes
Prayer songs competing at the other spectrum
Blaring speakers with speeches and messages.

Lane yesterday, one way today, a routed mayhem
Railway transit, foot-boarding buses, scurrying cabs
Cycle gaps, auto races, pedestrian nightmares hasten
Mad rushing office crowd, messy foot filled paths
The chiding parents chasing and tagging lazing kids

Artistic silk shades donned by the traditional and orthodox
The scent of *Malli*, hand-woven with daft, pace and care
Riveting dames from clans unmatched, on a giggle spree
Screeching bikes from a future generation, running scot-free
Youthful spirits with lighter bags that carelessly revel in tees
Studious opposite that break and buckle under pressure
Tales of mighty dreams coming true of common street folk

Blessing and cursing the authorities on beat
Jams and signals snake away in their time
Pedestrians break the jinx of foot crime
Half-dressed heroes, rowdies on the roads
Scaring the morning spirits with stares and abuses
Free bathing creatures, dressing on the streets
Forecasts and reports headline on hoardings
Concerned are the veterans, aged and retired

Young blood on the brink of a holiday if it pours
If it does, choking drains overflow, falls from hell
The humidity that defines the city even on the map
Killing the don of scents, talcum and eyeliners at dawn

First-day-first-show, celebrating the silver screen demi gods
The *Chepauk* lore, a pitch full of history and records
Concertos and Exhibitions, at *Sabhas* with invitation to spend
Art festivals, dramas, record dances, galleries galore
Area festivals, temple chariots, speakers and mikes
Goddesses revered, so are the priests and parties
Band of musicians, celebrate in birth or death
Garlanding statues, with cause to create chaos
Wedding parades, sudden rallies, paraded convoys
Undercurrent of caste, strata and race with divided lines

Window shopping dream brands in overflowing malls
Race courses, pool tables, gambling hubs, hidden ploy
Pirated goods, customs clearance, tight lipped, under table
Rare encounters in settlements aside the sea

Emerging infrastructure and towers on wastelands
Investments and promises that run this land
Grounds with dreams of talent and quotas
From marble bets to tourneys of *Mangaathaa*

Varying salaries from road to floors in concrete jungles
Rising cost of seats, educational or political
Business magnates, from all sizes and directions
Robbing the sanity of a normal day
Stealing the limelight of a madman's say.

All said and done, dealt and dusted
Once you check-in and sell your soul to this city
Bury the beating heart when you check-out

This city will love you to death, so will you till death
A city many hate to love...*Evvlo bet?*

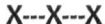

X---X---X

Nail the Enigma

1ne

Saga of the fall scripted in transparent ink
Immortal and disappear with light's one wink
An orchestra on stage with sound of black and grey
The gods are in tears when they see us pray

2wo

Sanity broken by a murderous tangent
Contoured map with endless routes
Wrinkled rubber of age-old routine
Tanned tales and colored rules

Th3

Orchestrated by pounding instrumentation
Scripted from ages and performed till day
Staged to set free ones arrested emotions
Feet are hurting but in pain you must sway

4our

She arrives and departs unannounced, an immortal she is
To touch and trigger by whispers in my ear, an art she is
Spills them through my eyes and hands, a life she is
Live or die, wait and rust, love she is…

Fi5e

Sorcerers Diabolique with strings attached, performing on stages galore
Commanding thy attention with light & sound, seething & screaming notes
Sender of waves, bringer of smoke, keeper of souls & giver of breath
Tribal beats bleeding with riffage, scales aplenty tattooed with a lore
of death

Si6

Level playing field, mapped till the eyes can see a rupture
Limitless possibilities, till words become wired to explode
A distant future where dreams become one's reality eventually
A time when Earth welcomes and is welcomed to another galaxy

Se7en

A barren desert with circling flames
The nomadic heart that beats a lone rhythm
An empty paper with a story to tell
A temple of gods with no priest to bell

Ei8ht

Is this the end of it all...without the start?
Are there no words for me...with that silence?
Do I have to try your patience...with violence?
Or does it take the rain to wipe your tears away?

Ni9e

Lover of the blue marble, the humming and hovering bee in absolute black
Poetry in motion, lyrical ballad in orbit, pearl in the shadow, an eternal halo
The fading smile of the Cheshire cat, staging scene of the romantic's act
Beholder of billion diamonds, oceanic symphony conductor in a flow

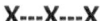

X---X---X